First published in Great Britain in 2024 by Wren & Rook
Text copyright © Hodder & Stoughton Limited 2024

Cover and inside artwork from Shutterstock.com

ISBN: 978 1 5263 6693 1

1 3 5 7 9 10 8 6 4 2

MIX
Paper | Supporting
responsible forestry
FSC
www.fsc.org FSC® C104740

Wren & Rook
An imprint of
Hachette Children's Group
Part of Hodder & Stoughton
Carmelite House
50 Victoria Embankment
London EC4Y 0DZ

An Hachette UK Company
www.hachette.co.uk
www.hachettechildrens.co.uk
Printed and bound in Great Britain by Clays Ltd, Elcograf S.p.A.

With thanks to Abigail McMahon.

CRIMSON ANGEL MERCY

THE ULTIMATE GUIDE TO
LOVE AT FIRST BITE

Contents

This book is written for
vamps finding vamps,
but all of the advice can
work for non-bloodsuckers
too. So, whether you're a
vampire looking for love,
or just a human struggling
to navigate red flags, then
there is advice for you too.

LOVE AT FIRST BITE

Hello, immortal lovers,

Welcome to my pulse-quickening, heart-wrenching guide to the supernatural dating world. Are you looking for love and coming up with dust? Are you searching for the alluring vampire of your dreams, but only coming across warty warlocks, soul-draining zombies and werewolves who smell faintly of wet dog? I know that there is a pale and interesting bloodsucker out there for you, lurking in the partial shadows with a brooding look on their face, and I'm here to tell you how to get them (and which ones to let go).

Think of this as your go-to guide for all supernatural love affairs, and me, Crimson Angel Mercy, as your personal advisor on all things that go bump in the night. There's nothing I don't know when it comes to lovers who bite!

Truly, who understands love? Well, by the end of this book, you! I'm going to talk you through the **five love languages**: words of affirmation, quality time, acts of service, physical touch, and gift giving and receiving. I'll define the love languages for you, sharing insights into the wants and needs of each one. We'll discuss how to dodge dating traps, spot ominous omens and find the right love language for you and your boo. But don't worry, love languages aren't literally another language. They're all about how you show your loved ones you care and how they show it back to you.

Plus, there will be plenty of quizzes to help you identify your ideal date outfit, decide which type of dater you and your friends are and even find the undead of your dreams. And I'll answer all my despairing readers' agony aunt problems and give you, dear reader, all the dos and don'ts of paranormal dating.

I am a big believer in the saying that 'knowledge is power'. If you know that vampires have moved to your area, then you won't be surprised when your friends start feeling a little drained. And if you know what romantic behaviour makes you weak at the knees – and which moves leave you colder than the grave – you'll be ready to take charge of your love life.

LOVE SPEAKS IN FIVE LANGUAGES

Now, before we dive into the depths of your heart and uncover your deepest and darkest (I hope!) secrets, I'd better explain the five love languages. They are words of affirmation, quality time, acts of service, physical touch, and gift giving and receiving.

For example, perhaps you get the warm fuzzies when someone gives you a compliment, but you're not a big fan of PDA. That would make words of affirmation one of your love languages. Or maybe you feel the opposite! An embrace might send tingles to your toes, but you aren't very good with your words. You're all about physical touch. Everyone feels an affinity with at least one love language, but most people show their love and appreciation using more than one method, so you might discover that a couple of the love languages work for you.

WHAT ARE THE QUALITIES OF EACH LOVE LANGUAGE?

Words of affirmation

QUALITIES	ACTIONS
Empathetic	Compliments
Active listener	Love notes
Encouraging	Long conversations
Affirming	

Quality time

QUALITIES	ACTIONS
Focused	Amazing dates
Savours the moment	One-on-one time
The organiser	Adventures

Acts of service

QUALITIES	ACTIONS
Trustworthy	Favours
Dependable	Support
Willing to go the extra mile	Helping out

Physical touch

QUALITIES	ACTIONS
Warm	Hand holding
Embracing	Hugs
Talks with their body	Kisses

Gift giving and receiving

QUALITIES	ACTIONS
Generous	Personalised gifts
Giving	Thoughtful ideas
Good memory for detail	Handmade cards

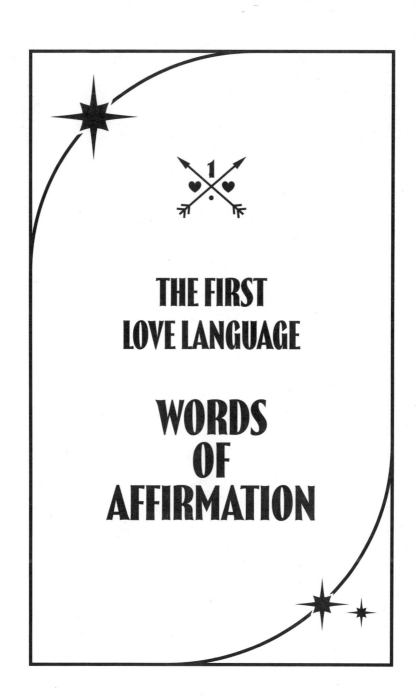

THE FIRST
LOVE LANGUAGE

WORDS
OF
AFFIRMATION

Do you find yourself seeking constant reassurance from your mysterious boo – and wishing you didn't have to ask for it? Or are you a little overwhelmed by the conversations about feelings instigated by your SO?

Then this chapter is for you! It's all about firsts. From what to do when you first get a crush on someone and making the first move, to falling in love for the first time – or even out of it.

Practising words of affirmation is all about saying how you feel to your bloodsucking bae.

Don't make them use their mind-reading skills; tell them they're *wonderful!*

Words of affirmation can be broken up into five categories:

APPRECIATE. Always remember to say 'fangs for everything' when they do something nice for you. Be loud and proud about how much they mean to you and the A-positive impact they have on your life.

ENCOURAGE. Be their biggest cheerleader, not their slayer. **Tell them when they excel and when you can see how hard they've been trying.**

AFFIRM. Assure them that their feelings and actions are valid. **Let those compliments flow!**

EMPATHISE. Understand their perspective, even when you don't share their experience. For example, although your parents have never attempted to get you to join their centuries-old and probably evil secret society, you can sympathise with your crush's feelings of frustration when this happens to them.

LISTEN ACTIVELY. Engage with your crush's conversation.
Maintain eye contact, listen to what they're saying and don't get distracted by your device (or by wondering how their hair remains so perfect even after they've super-sped to meet you).

HOW DO YOU KNOW IF YOUR LOVE LANGUAGE IS WORDS OF AFFIRMATION?

I know what you're thinking. How can you know what your love language is if you've never been in love or had a relationship? Or maybe you have experienced those things but still aren't sure.

Think about the other loves in your life. Any time you express your affection for your friends or family, you're probably using your preferred love language. What's your go-to way of sharing your fondness for them?

Here are some clues that might hint that your love language is words of affirmation:

- **You're a compliment machine!** You're the first to say when someone's new look suits them or if they've been a great friend.

- **You are very empathetic.** You are great at putting yourself in others' shoes; even if you haven't shared the same experiences, you always try to see their perspective.

- **You don't take anyone for granted and you make sure they know it.** You will always say thank you no matter how small the favour or gesture.

- **Your stationery collection is huge!** You don't care if it's old-fashioned, you love a handwritten letter! Notes of thanks, cute postcards, long sticker-covered letters to friends who just live round the corner . . . you're always writing.

- **You have a great memory for detail about other people's lives.** You listen to what they say, and you will remember it the next time you see them. You're the one who asks how a test went or whether they're feeling better, even if it was only mentioned in passing.

Basically, if you're a great communicator, then your love language might just be **words of affirmation.**

Learning another love language

Falling for a vampire may mean learning another language – and I don't mean Transylvanian. Maybe words are not your thing, but you know they mean everything to your crush.

Here is a practical guide to words of affirmation for those who need to know.

Complimenting someone's appearance is entry-level flirting. You might worry it's too basic, but trust Crimson, it's a classic for a reason. 'You look good today' is a strong starter compliment. It's even better to give your crush a specific compliment that shows you've paid attention. Comment on their new shoes or romantically windswept hair. I have a weakness for dark and fiery eyes. It's always the first thing I compliment and then let myself get lost in . . .

Call out the times your crush made you think, ***Wow, you're so interesting.*** Hearing that you noticed and valued their efforts will make them feel affirmed. Say, 'I loved the playlist you made me' or, 'I was so impressed when you used your super-strength to save that kitten'.

If you're not a natural sweet talker, then you can borrow some charm from a master like me. The words don't have to be original as long as you really mean the sentiment (and you don't try to pretend that you wrote them).

- **Send them a song lyric or quote that made you think of them** – and explain why it reminded you of them. Whether it's a classic love song or something a bit more nuanced, they'll appreciate that it made you think of them.

- **Don't keep the compliments between the two of you.** Share the love – tell your friends about a cool thing your crush did. Even better, tell your friends in front of your crush. This will amplify how flattered they feel at your thoughtful words and provide an opportunity for your friends to add their own compliments.

- **Remember a detail from a past conversation you had** – their favourite blood type, for example – and refer to it at a later date.

You are

loved

Like a stake through the heart

We all have weaknesses. For some, its direct sunlight, silver jewellery or particularly pointy sticks. For lovers of words of affirmation – human or otherwise – it's words that are our weak point. The right words make us feel great! And the wrong words, or in some cases no words at all, give us the ick. Discover what you should avoid harder than garlic if you want to impress your crush who cares about words.

Negging

Negging is the act of giving a backhanded compliment. A genuine compliment might be something like, 'Your velvet cape really suits you.' The backhanded version of that compliment would be, 'Your velvet cape would really suit you if it was a bit shorter.' Compliments that come with 'ifs', 'buts' or other qualifications don't make the recipient feel good. They make them feel inadequate.

Big effort, little response

One of the enhanced powers of lovers who give words of affirmation is that they always take notice of your thoughtful gestures. In return, they really like it when someone notices their own thoughtful gestures. And they feel very hurt if their own gestures go unnoticed or are not commented upon.

Not being authentic

Vampires are supernatural lie detectors. They can tell the moment you tell a lie, even a silly, small one, like pretending their favourite musician is yours too. They can hear your blood rushing and your heart beating faster. Your vampire crush values authenticity. They don't care if you disagree with them or if you don't have the same tastes as long as you're upfront and open with them.

VIBE CHECK
VAMPIRE EDITION

Your crush looks snatched, but you need to know more before you pledge your heart to the forces of darkness.

Take this quiz to discover who your type is.

YOU MEET . . .

A: At the cemetery. Lightning streaks the sky above you, illuminating a tall figure standing beside an ivy-covered crypt. Your heart skips a beat.

B: At a sports match. The crowd seems to part, revealing a hottie with a pained expression and furrowed eyebrows.

C: At the cinema. They prefer the dark and cool theatre despite it being a sunny day outside.

D: On stage at the local open mic slot. You sit, enraptured, as they play the soft boi classics.

E: In the classics section of your local bookshop. Your fingers brush as you both reach for *If We Were Villains*. You let them have it – you have two copies at home.

YOUR CRUSH'S STYLE IS . . .

A: Timeless. Or perhaps Time Lord. They're into slow fashion. So slow, they look like their style hasn't changed in several hundred years.

B: Relaxed. Loose tees, soft shirts, rugged boots. You can't spy any glitter on their garments but they somehow seem to sparkle.

C: Edgy. They rotate between their casual leather jacket, their going-out leather jacket and their finest leather jacket for special occasions.

D: Crumpled. They're more afraid of irons than they are of garlic. They accessorise their all-black look with dark glasses, even at night.

E: Autumnal. They wear an awful lot of layers for someone who doesn't seem to feel the cold.

YOUR FIRST DATE WAS . . .

A: A candlelit meal at their crumbling castle. Candlelight is sooo romantic, but . . . do they even have electricity?

B: A walk in the woods. It was so cute how they kept showing off by climbing trees – if tricky to hold a conversation.

C: Battling the forces of evil together. That is, the virtual forces of evil at the local arcade. You got the high score!

D: Listening to music at your local record store. You think they were trying to impress you – their hair was extra big that day.

E: Attending the latest exhibition at your local museum and glaring at your academic rivals from across the room. It's great to share hobbies!

RESULTS

Mostly As: Slicked-back hair, pointy collars, hint of an accent . . . you've fallen for a Classic Vampire!

Mostly Bs: This All-American Vampire is into trucks, plaid – and you!

Mostly Cs: You know you're the one to turn this frown upside down – the Dark 'n' Brooding Vampire has stolen your heart.

Mostly Ds: Is music the food of love? It is for this Soulful Rockstar Vampire.

Mostly Es: This hottie puts the crypt in cryptic – you've met a Dark Academia Vampire.

Dating disaster

You sit at the table with your crush. They've started to tell you a story but your phone flashes with a notification. Your bestie has commented fire emojis on your latest pic and you just have to like and reply. Besides, you're still listening. You can hear something about angry villagers . . . the terrible burden of immortality . . . wait. They've stopped talking.

You look up and your crush looks even more brooding than usual. Their brow is *really* furrowed and you're worried they're going to get stuck like that. They are upset with you and complain that you weren't listening properly. But you don't get it. You weren't talking, so that means you were listening. **Why are they so mad?**

Active listening

Listen up! **Listening is more than just not talking.** People who value words of affirmation also value a good listener. They don't enjoy feeling ignored, and they have a telepathic sense for when you're not giving them your full attention.

Try 'active listening', which is all about looking and sounding like you're giving your SO the attention they deserve.

Active listening is the act of fully engaging with what someone is saying. Active listeners hear what is being said, can decipher the secret clues hidden in body language and respond in a way that encourages further conversation.

Follow these tips on active listening and you'll warm even the coldest undead heart:

- **No distractions!** This means screens off, phone away, headphones off your head. It's time to give your crush the attention they deserve.

- **Look into their eyes.** Your date shouldn't have to use their vampiric mesmerism to get you to make eye contact. Making eye contact is an easy way to convey the fact you're really paying attention.

- **Encourage them to keep talking.** Non-verbal responses such as nodding your head or looking shocked are like IRL emojis. Your crush wants to know that you're paying attention, understanding what they're saying and keen to hear more about it.

♥ **Notice body language.** A good listener uses their eyes as well as their ears. You may pick up extra clues about how the speaker feels. For example, body language such as holding their arms close to their body, hunching over or fiddling with their hands may indicate that they feel uneasy.

Make your crush blush

So you've worked out that the way to your hottie's heart is through words of affirmation. But you don't share their love language. Does this mean you'll never speak the language of love together? Never fear, Crimson is here to help you get into their mind – and we won't even need telepathy to do it. Here is a list of genuine compliments that are guaranteed to make your crush's heart beat faster, even if it stopped beating centuries ago. These are just to help you get started – you should customise them to suit your boo.

Compliments make almost everyone feel good. However, the best ones focus on your boo's good choices.

Think styling their outfit, acting sweet or stretching to achieve their goals. Hearing you say, 'Your skin looks so sparkly when the sun shines' might feel fine, but it doesn't reflect their skills. An example of a flattering compliment might be: 'You are so good at vampire baseball.'

I have so much fun spending time with you.

No one makes me laugh like you do.

It was so impressive when you lifted that car.

You always make me feel valid.

You give great advice.

You're an amazing dancer.

I love hearing your take on things.

I feel so secure with you.

Do you have Ouija?

The problem with falling for a vampire is that they tend to be mysterious. This can mean that they often disappear for periods of time while they feud with their werewolf enemies, battle the forces of darkness or hide from their estranged siblings. You know, just vampire things. If the vampire you know is on social media, it's a great way to keep in contact, plus you get to see a snapshot of their interests and personality.

✦ **DON'T** feel like you have to join platforms you don't want to use just to stay in contact with them.

✦ **DO** like and comment on the posts that you enjoy. You won't build a connection just by stalking them.

✦ **DON'T** have a slip of the finger and accidentally like something from months ago when scrolling through old posts – cringe.

✦ **DO** slide into their DMs if you want to move from comments to conversations.

✦ **DON'T** open with a confession of how much you fancy them. Start with something lower stakes, such as mentioning their recent post.

✦ **DO** send them links to things you think you both might find funny and be interested in.

✦ **DON'T** spam them with messages if they don't reply.

✦ **DO** remember that not everyone is as they seem on social media. You only see what someone wants you to see.

MIND GAMES AND DARK ARTS

When you really like someone, it can be all-consuming, with your crush taking up residence in your head like a bat in the attic. You might start to think that you don't just want this person to like you back, you *need* them to like you back. But don't be fooled into thinking that turning your crush's head needs to be done using dark magic. There are much simpler ways to get their attention and still be yourself.

Should I wait to text back?

Everyone seems to think that if you message your crush back after one minute, it means you like them way more than they like you. Or if you message them five minutes after, then it means you like them the perfect amount. But if you reply after more than ten minutes, they'll think you don't like them at all and will never talk to you again. But guess what? The idea that there's a perfect amount of time to wait before replying to your crush's message is the number 3 vampire dating myth, right after soulmates and thinking it's at all acceptable to sneak into someone's room to watch them sleep (it isn't).

Some people like to message a lot and prefer to receive swift replies to their messages. Some people don't use their phone very much and don't want to spend a lot of time exchanging messages. Do what feels right to you, and tweak it to suit your crush's communication style if you want to.

Illusions and glamours

You might ask yourself: *How can I just be myself? What if my crush realises that I don't know much about death metal or that my sense of humour isn't as dry as theirs? Wouldn't it be better to hide that side of me so they only see my 'good' side?*

Pretending to be someone you're not is a trap! If your crush falls for this person, then you're stuck beneath this glamour forever. Which means you're stuck listening to music you don't like and never sharing the jokes you want to share. What a drag! If your crush doesn't like who you really are – embarrassing song choices and all – then they're not the one for you.

The follow, the like and the streak

Telling someone you like them is scary. They might share that they like you too (amazing!) or they might not feel the same way (cringe). You may wonder, on those moonless nights when your insecurities grow with the shadows, whether it would be easier if your crush just sort of . . . found out that you liked them without you ever having to tell them.

Couldn't you just send subtle messages by following their socials, liking all of their posts and uploads and building streaks? This way, if they don't like you back, then you never actually said the words – you have plausible deniability.

I'm sorry to tell you that this is more sham magic. There's a possibility that your crush might read between the lines of your excellent TikTok curation, your impeccable comment turnaround time and your subtle-but-not-really reposts and understand that you're telling them you think they're cute.

But there's a big chance that while you're hitting that like button, wondering why your crush hasn't realised you think they're the best, they might be wondering what it all really means . . .

Follow, like and interact with them all you like. After all, it's a great way to get to know them. But if you want them to know that you like them, there's only one way to do it . . . tell them!

COMMUNICATION

There are a lot of challenges when dating a vampire. Whether that's only being able to go on dates on very cloudy days, not being able to take mirror selfies or having to avoid eating anywhere that the food includes garlic (impossible), there are a lot of obstacles. One way to make life – and undeath – easier for yourselves is to have a good foundation of healthy communication. **Healthy communication is important for any relationship, whatever your preferred love language is.**

Healthy communication isn't just about checking in with each other at the end of a busy day – or night. It's about being brave and honest when sharing your thoughts and feelings.

Practise these basic rules and you'll be the couple everyone else aspires to be:

1. **Tell your partner what you like and don't like.** For example, don't silently hope they'll hold your hand – reach out and hold their hand! And tell them that hand holding is something you like to do. And if you're not big on PDA? Tell them that too!

2. **Listen to what your crush likes and doesn't like.** This means not trying to talk them out of their opinion when you disagree with it. Try to understand their point of view instead. You may be confused about how to be 'fair' when one of you likes something and the other one doesn't. Try to use the 'two yeses' rule. This means that both partners have to say yes to an activity or a behaviour. For example, if you say yes, you do want to see the latest spooky film, but your vampire crush says no because they're a big scaredy bat, then seeing that film together is off the table. Go to see the film with your brave bestie instead and pick something that both you and your crush enjoy watching.

3. **Understand that feelings and opinions can change.** It's OK to change your mind about something and to tell your crush about it. And it's OK for them to change

their mind too. However, remember, *no compelling.* The only mind you can change is your own.

4. **Two people set the rules.** Everybody communicates differently – that's what learning the love languages is all about! For example, think about how you prefer to argue. Some people like to talk everything through all in one go. They don't want to stop until the argument reaches a resolution and they feel bad if the conversation ends without one. Other people can become overwhelmed with feelings and need to take breaks when arguing in order to process them. Neither person is wrong; they're just different.

5. **Building trust is perfectly normal.** Being honest doesn't mean you have to share everything about yourself all at once! It's acceptable to share more about your thoughts and feelings as your connection grows. You may wish to know someone a bit better before you tell them all your private thoughts and feelings. Whenever it feels right to you, then it's right to do.

Dating disaster

Is your crush a vampire or a werewolf?

You go on a date with your crush and they are soooo sweet. They laugh at all your jokes, they're into your conversation and they do that cute tucking-a-strand-of-hair-behind-your-ear thing. But towards the end of the date, you bump into some IRL mutual friends. Then everything changes. Your date won't hold your hand and instead of laughing with you, they make you the butt of the joke.

Or perhaps whenever you both spend time with other people, your crush has nothing but good things to say to you. But then will privately send you mean messages or is always telling you that you've done something wrong.

You're confused. **What happened to the sweet romantic you thought you knew?**

Cursed to transform

What a terrible tail – I mean, tale. I'm sorry to say you haven't fallen for a vampire. The situation is far hairier. You've fallen for a werewolf. The signs are all there: they appear to be nice, down to earth and so into you some of the time. But come the full moon, or a moment of privacy or another trigger, and they turn into a complete beast!

That's NOT OK. It is not enough for someone to be kind to you only some of the time. A werewolf is still a werewolf, even when they look and act like a human. It's time to put a silver bullet in that relationship the moment they start to be mean.

It can be hard to know how to respond when someone says something nasty to you. Who hasn't had that 'aha' moment two days later when you think of a great witty comeback? Here are a few scripts to have locked and loaded in case you encounter another werewolf:

> *Hey! I don't like it when you say things like that. Please stop.*

> *I feel bad when you say things like that. Can you not talk to me like that in the future?*

Some werewolves like to pass off their mean comments as jokes. Don't let them try to make you feel as though you can't take a joke. After all, a joke has to be funny to both the teller and the listener. Don't feel pressured into brushing it off because you don't want to seem like you don't have a sense of humour. **You do!**

Slay squad

Do you have main character energy or are you serving sidekick in your own life? There's a rag-tag squad of besties and frenemies at the heart of every supernatural romance. The nerdy one, the funny one, the mean but secretly nice one . . . they support each other through thick and thin. Gather your best ghoulfriends and play this game of 'who's most likely to', to see who's who in your squad.

Who is most likely to. . .
- Fall for a vampire?
- Crack a joke at the WRONG moment?
- Be a secret witch?
- Prefer studying to romance?
- Say 'there's a logical explanation for this'?
- Start some drama?
- Go monster hunting in the middle of the night?
- Be the first to say, 'break up'!
- Be mistaken for a vampire themselves?
- Faint at the sight of blood?
- Trip over a gravestone?
- Always have a witty one-liner on the tip of their tongue?

Have I found my soulmate?

Dating a vampire can be so dramatic. Between the enemies leaping out from behind every bush, tearful confessions about being a bloodsucker (which you had already guessed because, duh) and friends-turned-family-turned-enemies-turned-friends-again who may or may not want to kill you . . . how can you tell whether you're feeling butterflies in your stomach or just a hefty rush of adrenaline? **Is this a crush? Or is it something more?**

We use the word 'love' to cover the feelings we have in all sorts of different relationships. But there are many different types of love. One is the love felt for family members.

Sometimes this is a pure, Cullen-style love; other times it's a twisted love, but all the stronger for being so twisted – à la the Mikaelson clan.

Of course, there's also the love we share with our friends. Love between friends is strong and burns brightly. It illuminates our souls and keeps us warm through our troubles – evil doppelgangers, secret societies, the occasional apocalypse, even a driving test. It's the love that binds any Scooby gang together.

There's even a difference between the types of love that occur in relationships. One category is 'playful' love, known as a crush. Then there is an intense love involving attraction – when a crush has deepened into a heated connection. After that, there is a love that occurs when two people have been committed to each other for a long time.

It's a question older than your crush's Grandad Vlad's castle. Are the feelings you're experiencing lust or something more? Compare your feelings for your fanged object of affection to your existing loving relationships. Do your feelings match those for your friends? For your family? Are they comfortable and strong but no butterflies? Or are your feelings all butterflies but no trust and security? Perhaps you feel a combination of the two – that may be love!

Dear Crimson,

I've been in a talking stage for two weeks and I'm absolutely sure that I've found the one! All my friends say that it's too soon for me to be in love, but I know that's what I'm feeling. Is it too soon to drop the L bomb?

Fang Lover

Dear Fang Lover,

There are no hard and fast rules about falling in love, but saying I love you after two weeks might be a tad too keen. Some people are very quick to fall in love and maybe your bloodsucker feels the same. But don't get lust and love confused. If you say that you have fallen, then I believe you, but are you a hundred per cent sure what you're feeling is a deep connection, or do you just fancy the pants off your new boo?

You're still in a talking stage with this hottie. The talking stage is the very first step on the dating

journey and preludes a committed relationship. You're both still having fun and getting to know each other. You might find, with a bit more time, that you can't stand the way they chew their food or speak to waiters, and they might find, well . . . someone else. So take your time exploring those feelings – there's nothing worse than jumping the gun with the love bomb and being met with silence. It's deafening . . .

How would you feel if you declared your love (rose petals and all) and didn't hear them back? If you feel secure enough to know you're in a situation where you have more feelings than your other half, then go ahead, stand underneath their window and shout from the rooftops. However, if you think that not having your feelings returned yet might make you feel rejected, it might be better to wait until your relationship has developed further. At least until you've been on a few dates.

Always here to serve,
Crimson

Love and other tricky stuff

There are lots of other words you might want to use when you're falling in lust. You might find yourself wanting to affirm your connection by asking, *'Is this more than just teaming up to defeat our immortal enemies?'* or, *'Do you care for me as much as you care about coffins?'* Regardless of what words of affirmation you might be saying, the one thing you don't have to say is 'I love you' just because they've said it to you.

Here are some suggestions for what you can say to your love interest when they confess their undying love for you.

💜 For when you're falling but not fallen:
  - *I'm falling for you too.*

💜 For when you're feeling good but it's not that deep:
  - *I'm not there yet but I have so much fun spending time with you.*

  - *I'm not there yet but I think you're an amazing and special person.*

❤ For when you don't know how you feel yet:
- ***Thank you for telling me how you feel.***

- ***I need a few days to process that. Thanks for being so open with me.***

❤ For when they say it way, way too soon:
- ***I like you a lot but I think we need to get to know each other better.****

*You don't have to say that you like them a lot if that's not how you feel. It's perfectly acceptable to tell them you need more time getting to know each other before you confess your love for them.

Bloodsucker moment

What happens when you confess your feelings and in return you get . . . not exactly a no? But not really a yes? What does your crush mean when they say things like . . .

- I'm not ready to be in a relationship.

- I'm cursed and all my relationships are doomed to fail.

- I wouldn't treat you well.

- I'm not a good person.

- I'm attracted to you but I don't want to be with you.

- It's not a good time to be in a relationship as I'm locked in a battle of wits with my immortal and vengeful ex for all eternity.

The heart is a very hopeful organ. None of the phrases above are an exact 'no'. So, when your crush says to you, 'I'm not ready to be in a relationship', that hopeful heart of yours might hear, 'When I'm ready, I will be in a relationship with you'. You hear the words, 'I'm not a good person', but your heart might whisper, 'They're just saying that to be humble'. You hear, 'I'm too busy battling the forces of darkness both in the world and within my own soul', but your heart says, 'Let's help them out with their burdens and then they'll want to be with us'.

Listen up, all you hopeful hearts! Sometimes a 'no' will sound like a 'maybe'. Why wouldn't they just be direct and say 'no'? Perhaps the person doesn't want to hurt your feelings. It takes guts to tell someone something they don't want to hear. Or maybe there's a darker reason, like they enjoy playing mind games. Either way, it's best for you to hear anything other than an enthusiastic yes as a truthful no.

My undead romance died…

Dear Crimson,

I've been talking to the sweetest vampire. We have the same twisted sense of humour, we are obsessed with the same artist online, we click well IRL and we talk all the time. Or at least we did. My boo has stopped replying to my messages!

I've tried everything to get them to reply. I reached out casually a few times, then I apologised for anything I did wrong ,and recently I sent them a long message explaining how much this hurts me and that I just want closure.

I can't stop obsessing over them. I check my phone all the time. Every time I get a notification my heart skips a beat, but it's never them.

What's going on? Did a werewolf eat their phone? Did the latest iOS update contain a hex? Why did they stop talking to me? How can I make them reply?

Yours,
Missing My Soulmate

Dear Missing,

Ouch! It sounds like you've been ghosted.

That. Sucks.

When you've been ghosted, you don't just lose the person you've really connected with but you're left with lots of questions. *Why have they cut me out? What went wrong? How can I fix it?* This is a lot of unfinished business that deepens the hurt and turns it into an obsession.

You've asked two questions: why did they stop talking to you, and how can you make them reply?

Here's one of my arcane secrets: *the why doesn't matter.* The fact is, they've made a decision to exclude you from their life and no explanation they could give you would make you feel much better about the situation. The *why* could be simple. One ghost feels the spark sputter but is too afraid to speak up. Another ghost feels overwhelmed by life and opts to drop their talking stage. Their *why* was

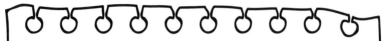

different but their *how* was the same: instead of communicating with their new flame, they blinked them out of existence.

I'm sorry, Missing. Your boo has taken your relationship to the ghost realm and there are no magic words that will get you your final reply. In fact, their silence is their last message to you. They're saying, 'Please don't contact me'. Even though you feel hurt by that message, you need to respect that. It's time to stop messaging them and find the closure you need.

Being temporal, ghosts can't even close a gate, let alone a relationship. Only you can find closure. It's time to stop waiting around for your ghoul and start going through the classic break-up moves. Spend time with your friends, do your favourite activities and indulge in some of your favourite foods. Do anything other than waste time thinking about this ghoulish ghoster.

Always here to serve,
Crimson

Help! My ghost has become a poltergeist!

Have you ever closed a cupboard door only to find it open again moments later? Been alone in your home but felt a prickly feeling on the back of your neck? Left your shoes in one spot and found they've moved to another part of your home? You may have encountered a real-life poltergeist. A poltergeist is a ghost that has a physical presence. Although you never see them, you can feel them interacting with the world around you.

A poltergeist can also be an ex who disappeared from your life, then later started orbiting you. An orbiting ex never contacts you directly. Instead, they like your posts and view your stories. They do just enough for you to know they're still around. On the surface it seems as though they are respecting your break-up. However, because they're always liking and following, you never have the pleasure of just being able to forget about them. You feel watched.

When is the right time to perform an exorcism? Whenever you like! Words aren't enough to exorcise a poltergeist. The engagement feeds them and gives them the response that they were fishing for. You need to spring into action. Don't feel as though you have to wait for your ex to do something explicitly 'wrong' or to break some unspoken law of ex-dom. If you don't want to be orbited, then you don't have to be orbited. **Hit the block button and exorcise the poltergeist!**

Blood relatives

Telling your family that you have a boyfriend or a girlfriend is scary enough, let alone telling your family you have a vampire partner. However, if you have a positive relationship with your family, you'll be thinking about how to share the good news. How do you pick the right time to introduce the two sides of your life? There are a few factors you can take into consideration to make the daunting process go more smoothly.

- **Bring everyone up to speed.** Ideally your parents should know they're about to meet your partner, and your partner your parents, before everyone arrives at the same destination. Communication is key to making sure everyone knows what's going on. There's nothing more awkward than your vampire lover being taken by surprise, turning into a bat and flapping off into the moonlight.

- **Timing is everything.** And I'm not just talking about making sure your vampire partner doesn't get dusted in a ray of sunlight. Stressful periods, such as exam time, pressure at work or during a family illness, can lead to stressed people. And stressed people do not make good first impressions! Pick a moment when you don't have any big deadlines or life events on the calendar and you can just focus on the meeting ahead.

- **Start small.** Vampires always feel calmer in low-stakes situations. The fancier and more complicated the event, the more pressure is felt by everyone. Avoid introducing your partner to the family at big occasions such as large parties, big birthdays or similar. Think short and sweet, such as meeting before you go on a date or grabbing coffee together.

- **Think about how all the parties involved best receive information.** Use your words of affirmation to reassure an anxious partner and to explain how you want your family to approach them. This always helps everyone feel calmer upon meeting.

THE SECOND
LOVE LANGUAGE

QUALITY
TIME

Do you hate it when your friends spend all your time together trying to get snaps for socials? Are you wondering how to balance your time between friends, family, saving the world and your new boo?

Then it's **quality time** that really speaks to you. If spending time together is at the centre of your idea of a good relationship, whether that be an emerging fling with your boo-to-be or a committed relationship with a creature of the night, then this is the chapter for you. But before we get started, let's break down the absolute essentials of the quality time love language into bite-sized pieces:

TOGETHERNESS. Banish the phones. Sign out of socials. Put all distractions to one side and focus solely on the time you're sharing with your boo.

COMMITMENT. Put some respect on your boo's time. Be the person that shows up for them on time and isn't always rearranging.

PLANNING. A quality-time lover sees all the effort that goes into planning a great date and hears, 'I like you a lot!'

QUALITY. It's literally in the name! One really good date is way better than five rushed ones.

HOW DO YOU KNOW IF YOUR LOVE LANGUAGE IS QUALITY TIME?

You may have noticed that you are more comfortable expressing yourself with actions rather than words. Perhaps a compliment makes you feel self-conscious, and you feel more awkward than flattered. But spending time with your boo, whether that's patrolling the graveyard for bad guys or grabbing a bite at the local café, really sets off fireworks in your body.

If someone asked you what the nicest thing anyone has ever done for you was, your top answers would all involve your besties and loved ones.

Here are a few other signs that you seek out quality time:

· Every time you add something fun to your to-do list, **you immediately think of the person you'd like to do that activity with.**

· **Spending time with other people is your priority!** You will go out of your way to spend time with friends and romantic interests.

· **You're like a social solar panel.** You leave quality time with friends and loved ones feeling like you have the vigour of a newly turned vamp. On the flip side of that . . .

· **You're quick to feel lonely.** If too many days pass without seeing your besties in person, then you feel sad. You're better in a pack, not as a lone wolf.

· **You're the organiser of the group.** You scope out fun activities, check the weather for risk of sun exposure and book the tickets. It's not always easy but it is always worth it.

· **Your ideal date is all about interaction.** You're not so keen on dates where you can't talk, like the cinema or a museum. You want to get to know your date, not sit in silence.

· **Long-distance relationships are not your thing.**

Learning another love language

Even if this doesn't sound like the love language for you, let's shapeshift into someone who prizes quality time and see the world through their eyes, so we can be better at romancing them. Close your eyes. Take a deep breath. Open them again. You're seeing romantic walks, you're seeing long conversations filled with laughter, you're seeing . . . bookmarked perfect date ideas, mood boards and spreadsheets? And the spreadsheets are colour coded?! There's more organisation involved in quality time than you expected.

Here's where you can step in and wow them.

- **Organise some of the dates.** Those with quality time at their core often take charge. They make the suggestions, they chase the RSVPs, they book the tickets. They value spending time together so much that they're willing to put the effort in. They even like it! But that doesn't mean they want to be the only person making the effort. If you arrange the date, they'll see it as you showing that you care and will probably go all heart-eyed over it.

- **The emphasis should be on spending time together.** You don't need to fly them to Paris for dinner on top of the Eiffel Tower or take them to your family crypt filled with hundreds of candles. It just needs to be something you'll both find fun and enjoy. No need to post about it on socials.

- **Keep it simple.** Quality time is about the time you have together, not whether it's packed full of activities. Your date loves climbing? Great. Book some time at the rock wall (although their super-strength might not require them needing any gear). They're not big on eating? Fine, go between meals. Just enjoy the time you have together, even the lulls. Those quieter moments can lead to real silliness, or deep conversations, or unexpected events – these are all examples of the authentic connections that quality-time lovers appreciate.

Like a stake through the heart

Of course, there are some complications to spending quality time with a vampire lover. They're a night owl; you value your sleep. They can't enter a human's home uninvited by the owner; you're not sure whether you're ready for them to meet your parents. They're barred from walking on sacred ground; you've been dying to try that new coffee shop called The Holy Roast. But you guys can make it work! You just have to be aware of the following pitfalls, as they really throw holy water on the flames of romance for the quality-time crazed . . .

Cancellations

If a date makes a quality-time crush feel good, then a cancelled date makes them feel bad. Someone who loves spending quality time together interprets a cancellation as a message that says, 'You are not the priority'. They'd rather you were honest and upfront, and decline a date, than you say yes and then drop them when other plans come along.

Unfocused

When someone who values quality time is on a date, they're completely there. Their focus is entirely on their crush. That means headphones off, no phones, no dashing off to catch up with mysterious frenemies who have popped up out of the blue. They like to do activities together, but not if they come at the expense of conversation and interactions.

The monster mish-mash

Your quality-time practitioner is sensitive to unclear priorities. They are happy for you to have a busy lifestyle full of hobbies and friends, but they want to be part of it too. For example, if you love playing games, then invite them over for a board-game night so you can enjoy your hobby together. But if you spend a lot of time away from home at tournaments make sure to prioritise spending time with them when you're back – or even invite them along!

Make your crush blush

Need some help translating the language of quality time to sweep a date-loving vampire off their feet? If this doesn't come naturally to you, then here's a list of great date suggestions to start with. Hopefully they spark a few other ideas for you too.

> Whether your crush is a fan of fancy meals or crazy for countryside walks, there's one thing that all these date ideas have in common: keeping your attention focused on your date. Commit to putting your phone away. Or, if you can't go without it for so long, or your date is into snapping pics with you, then impose a limit on yourself before you get there.

Art or light trail

Art trails are the perfect way to coax a moody artistic vampire out of their candlelit studio, even if it's only to make biting comments about all the art. Culture, fresh air, wonderful company – what could be better?

Stargazing

This is the perfect date for a vampire in so many ways. It's at night, so there's an extremely low risk of your boo being weakened by the sun. Plus, they can use their super-sight to spot falling stars. Dreamy. All you have to do is download an app featuring constellation maps and you're all set.

Board-game café

Playing a game with your boo means you are really focused. You're much less likely to be distracted by your phone when you have to pay attention to the rules. If there aren't any board-game cafés in your area, you can easily create one by . . . bringing a board game to a café! Most places won't mind as long as you purchase a drink or bite to eat while you're there. Tip: this isn't a date for sore losers.

Choose your date wisely

What's your boo's biggest weakness? Anyone familiar with supernatural lore knows that a creature blessed with phenomenal cosmic power will also be cursed with a crippling weakness. The more powerful the creature, the sillier the weakness. Witches? They might be able to wave their hands to light a candle, but they have all the weaknesses that humans do. Werewolves? Silver bullets (although most people are bothered by bullets). Vampires, however? Garlic. Running water. A sunny day. C'mon!

With that in mind, you need to plan your dates carefully. Here's my handy health and safety guide to the most popular types of date and the risks your boo might encounter there.

In-house hangout

This one should be simple. You invite your crush over, you hang out together, make some snacks, play a game and act goofy. Easy. Except . . . only the owner of the house can invite a vampire in. A bit tricky if you live with family or are renting.

RISK RATING: 3/10 – not the one!

Grabbing a bite to eat

Modern vampires have largely dropped the aversion to garlic. Perhaps they feel that being scared of a vegetable is bad for their rep. Still, being a garlic hater does make eating out a challenge. Japanese cuisine uses comparatively little garlic, so this may be your best bet.

RISK RATING: 4/10 – sushi it is!

Hikes, bikes and other outdoor activities

Some vampires have serious sunlight struggles. Others? Not so much. It's best to check your boo's comfort level with sunlight before planning a day trip to the beach. Once you've done that, keep a sharp eye on your weather app. Nothing kills the mood like your date poofing into a billion itsy pieces.

RISK RATING: 7/10 – cloudy with a chance of dusting.

On reflection…

Vampires don't have a reflection. The only real danger this causes them is the risk of an uncoordinated outfit, or the peril of not realising they have something stuck between their fangs. However, it can be pretty annoying for dates. Visiting the house of mirrors at a carnival is out. Photobooths are also out of the question.

RISK RATING: 1/10 – people will think you have an imaginary boo-friend.

Thrills and spills

OK, this one is a deep cut. We're talking from the vault. Apparently, if you spill a bag of rice or seeds in front of a vampire, they have to stop and count it all. Ancient folklore doesn't mention whether this counts for popcorn, perhaps because medieval peasants didn't make it to the movies very often. But still, perhaps just get a drink at the concession stand.

RISK RATING: 1/10 – while they're tidying you can watch the after-credits scene

Slay your style

Now you've locked down the time, the place and, most importantly, the person, it's time to focus on the look. It's as important as ever to look and feel yourself. And nailing the fit can be a massive boost for your confidence. Let's get you styled and set for the date ahead.

VAMPIRE FLEDGLING

Do you plan your fits to fit in or do you put the outsider in outfit?

FIT IN

OUTSIDER OUTFIT

You're a bit of a traditionalist when it comes to vampiric style: flowy white peasant shirts, big collars and even a daring cape or two. It's a bold first-date look, but you aren't afraid to be yourself.

Formalwear isn't really your style. You believe in the power of a good leather jacket. Fitted, oversized, sleek, weathered – there's a style for any date.

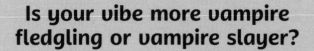

Is your vibe more vampire fledgling or vampire slayer?

VAMPIRE SLAYER

Are you a baddie with a battle axe or a savage sweetheart?

BADDIE

You like uplifted sportswear and street style with a twist. You don't get date-ready, you stay date-ready.

SAVAGE SWEETHEART

You may be ready to kick butt at a moment's notice, but that doesn't mean you need to shout about it. Soft silhouettes and sweet details are your style.

Dating decisions

Congratulations! You've been brave and asked your boo on a date – and they said yes. Or perhaps they asked you. You've already used my handy health and safety guide to ensure your date doesn't get dusted. Next, let's create an environment where romance can thrive by putting our (mad) scientist goggles on and calculating the perfect date.

Be yourself

When you think of dates, you might be thinking red roses and fancy meals, and that might be right for you. For others, it might mean a night patrolling the graveyard with hot dogs in hand. Forget what other people think your first date 'should' be – the single most important thing is that you've picked an activity you will both enjoy. But remember to think about the environment too. For example, say you both like art. A good date activity might be to visit an art gallery or museum exhibition. But say you both like art but you're also a self-confessed loudmouth. A quiet, reserved place like an art gallery might not be an environment where you can be yourself. What about a craft fair or Comic Con?

. . . Just yourself

Telling people when and where you're going on a date can be a smart move. You might even want to meet up with your friends shortly after and go over the date. Just don't bring your friends or family ON the date. And yes, having them lurk just out of sight counts! Make a rule between you and your crush – you won't invite your friends to crash as long as they don't allow their shady brother or mysterious maker to pop up when you least expect it.

Budget

Decide your budget ahead of time. Money can be such an awkward topic. Some people worry that not having much money makes them unattractive. Others don't like it if people flash their cash because they think that time has more value than money. Don't worry if your budget is zilch. Remember that the single most popular answer to the question, 'What's your ideal date?' is 'Long walks on the beach'. And that doesn't cost a thing (unless you're flying your boo to the beach).

Always know your escape route

OK, I'm being a bit dramatic. But not completely dramatic. In the world of vampire romance, the worst-case scenario for your first date might be that your would-be boo is revealed to be secretly evil, or you wander into werewolf territory by accident. But consider the non-life threatening scenario – the date sucks. A savvy dater will have arranged a date with an activity that has a firm end point, such as bowling, or will have established that they have to be home by a certain time. That way you can smile, say fangs for everything and leave that awkward date behind. If you're having lots of fun, you can always choose to extend the date.

Dating disasters
When first dates go wrong

First dates can feel high stakes. Even when you've been friends with your date, or you've had a long talking stage, or you're a generally confident person. You're hoping that you've picked the right activity, that you're wearing the right outfit, that the good vibes you felt between you continue and that nothing goes wrong.

But . . . what if something does go wrong? Will your crush think less of you? Will the spark die out? My guess is you'll find that something going wrong is never as bad as you think. **Let's run some POVs and find out:**

POV: You went on a date and there was no spark

OK, so it wasn't love at first bite. The flirting fell flat, the spark sputtered out, the banter was bust . . . I could go on. It's fine, these things sting, but the pain quickly fades. Firstly, let us take this moment to mourn what might have been. Dearly beloved, we are gathered here, etc. etc. Now it's time to move past the upset: blast some beats, shake it off with your friends and reset.

POV: You totally blanked

Did some passing vamp mind-wipe you on your way to your date? Because you went completely blank! All your amazing chat flew out of your mind like a bat out of – never mind. You'd been feeling the frisson before you met so you didn't expect to just sit in silence. Awkward. But it will only get more awkward if you don't acknowledge it. Shoot your boo-to-be a message explaining the date didn't go as you'd hoped, that for some reason you just blanked, and that you'd like to try again.

POV: You dropped a clumsy clanger

You tripped, or knocked over a glass, or dropped your bag. Don't worry. Have you ever seen a romcom? Clumsiness is the number-one most attractive flaw a person can have. Having witnessed your clumsiness, your date now has no choice but to fall deeply in love with you. Your love story will include several misunderstandings and end in a confession at an airport or the altar. Or . . . this incident, while causing a deep level of cringe in the moment, will eventually be forgotten, or at worst remembered as a funny anecdote.

Friend dates

Stepping into a new world of dating can be thrilling, but don't let it become all-consuming. What about your day ones? That's your coven. You'll be headed for major double, double, toil and trouble if you just abandon them at the first sign of romance. Sure, the regular hangouts are comforting and the group chat is thriving. But doesn't the squad deserve magic moments too?

That's why friend dates are as important as romantic dates. They're a time to reconnect and strengthen those bonds of friendship. Enjoy new experiences together, vent about dating, try something you've always wanted to or just step out of your daily routine. Go shopping, get your nails done or head to a rage room. Whatever it takes to make you feel better after a dating disaster.

Keep prioritising your friends even when you're busy going on romantic dates. Don't start breaking long-standing arrangements because your new boo has invited you for a walk in the woods. Most relationships aren't affected by the occasional rearrange. Things come up; sometimes the world needs saving. But your friends will care if you always cancel on them for a non-emergency meet-up with your crush.

This or that: Dating edition

Gather up the ghoulfriends for a classic game of this or that. What do you have in common and what do they like that makes you say, 'Wait, what?'. Who has a sweet tooth and who has a sharp tongue? Who is an old-school romantic and who is a heartbreaker?

Pick one answer from each pair of choices.

Cinema or arcade?
Graveyard picnic or haunted brunch?
Brawling werewolves or crashing a coven?
Live music or masquerade?
Moonlight kisses or anti-PDA?
Thrifting or designer shopping?
Street food or dessert café?
Graveyard or ruins?
Polaroid pics or reels?
Sweet nothings or bantering back and forth?
All-day hikes or dancing the night away?

Dear Crimson,

Can you help me settle an argument between me and my boo? Sometimes, I'm a little late to our dates. It's never usually more than fifteen minutes but they have started to get annoyed with me and keep asking why I am never on time.

Here's the thing. The area we live in may seem quiet and wholesome but it's absolutely riddled with hauntings, curses and supernatural creatures. Have you ever tried to catch the bus in a town built on a site of supernatural significance? I've heard all the usual jokes about late buses, but I would be so grateful if that was my problem. By the time I've made it to my date I've fought off two attempts on my life, exorcised a possessed bus driver and found what looked like a lost purse but turned out to be a cursed artefact.

Crimson, I'm tired. When I get to my date I just want to be in the moment with them. We never know how long we have before we realise the waitress is working for the Big Bad and we transition from holding hands to hand-to-hand combat.

Surely when you're a vampire who is going to live forever you can spare fifteen minutes to wait for a chronically late cutie like me?

Late But Great

Oh Late But Great,

It sounds like you have a love language mismatch with your boo. You think that fifteen minutes here and there shouldn't matter to a vampire with all the time in the world. But here's the thing. It does.

I think we have two problems to solve here. Firstly, you have to accept that being late is hurting your boo's feelings.

Secondly, it sounds like you have a much higher than average instance of run-ins with supernatural phenomena. Have you been to your doctors lately to ask whether you might have Chosen One syndrome? Symptoms include regular supernatural peril, unusually high instances of creature encounters and one or more vampire romances. If diagnosed you may be referred to a witch doctor, who will prescribe you wards and charms to help reduce unwanted encounters.

Now, I know that you have a lot on your plate. But, next time you run into trouble, try to give your partner a heads up that you are likely to be late. Proactive communication goes a long way to help hurt feelings. Instead of sitting around and twiddling their thumbs, your SO will at least have an idea of your new arrival time and your reason for being late.

Enable voice-to-text to send your message, for times you need to warn your boo you'll be late while fighting a group of vampiric henchmen. As a bonus your voice-to-text translator will probably pick up all the sound effects for added authenticity: 'Hey, just to let you know – take that, fang face – I've run into some trouble – would you stake your life on that – so my new eta will be fifteen minutes later – hah! I'm leaving you in the dust.'

Always here to serve,

Crimson

Dear Crimson,

I'm confused. I love spending time with my friends. I don't know how it's possible to have conversations that are somehow stupid, deep and hilarious all at once, but ours are. But there's a catch. I come away from our hangouts feeling drained. These guys are my squad and I know we're not drifting apart. They're some of the coolest human beings I know.

However, sometimes they invite me to hang out and my heart sinks. I don't know why? The plan always sounds really fun, whether we're chilling at someone's house or planning a big night out. I love everyone in the group. But, if I've spent a lot of time out of the house with people, or it looks as though my weekend is going to be really busy, there's something in me that wants to turn the invite down. Chilling in my home alone sounds amazing, like a cool flannel for my hot brain.

Why do I feel like this? Don't normal people want to spend time with their favourite people?

Weirding Myself Out

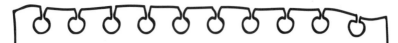

Hey, Weirdo,

There's nothing weird about you! Sooo many people feel the same way you do. You don't secretly hate your friends because you feel tired after spending time with them. You aren't strange because you prefer your weekend and holidays to have some rest time as well as play time.

Think of yourself as a tablet. You have two sources of power – two batteries. One provides physical energy and one provides mental energy. Almost everyone gets their physical energy from the same sources – food, drink and rest. And almost everyone runs their physical energy down in the same way – being awake and moving around. However, the things that fill up our mental-energy battery and the things that drain it are different for everyone.

Some people love being in the spotlight. Like me! If you hadn't noticed, I love speaking to people and hearing all about their lives. I feed off social energy

like I'm a vampire myself. However, I know loads of people for whom that would be a total nightmare. We love spending time with each other but we wouldn't want to swap places – they'd have empty batteries by lunchtime and I would never have the chance to recharge mine.

It sounds like you are an introvert. Don't worry, I'm not going to lock you up in a dark and stormy tower – you can still visit your friends. My advice? Listen to your instincts. If you've got an amazing day planned with your friends, remember to book in a 'recharge day' the next day. Say no to invites that fall on weekends where you already have something planned, unless it's something completely unmissable, like a birthday or a once-in-a-lifetime trip.

Always here to serve,
Crimson

Bloodsucker moment

My boo keeps arranging dates that are way out of my budget. Even my friends do it sometimes. What can I do?

A hundred years is a lot of time to build up an allowance. It's no wonder that your vampiric boo's idea of a cheap date might be a little bit different to yours. You're refreshing your money app hoping some cash will suddenly appear while they drop cash on takeaways (which they can't even eat). Add your money woes to the pressure of spending quality time with your boo and you might find yourself pressed and stressed.

Don't worry. Budgetary mismatches are common, even outside of vampire/human relationships. I have some tips and tricks to help you manage your money and still make the most of your quality time.

- **Be upfront.** Don't be embarrassed by money matters. Approach your SO or your friend group and let them know that you need to be careful with your cash. Keep it friendly but matter of fact. And don't apologise. Decide how you'd like to limit your spending. Would you like to splurge on one really fancy date once a month and otherwise keep your time limited to hangouts? Would you like to go out regularly but at lower-cost venues? My suggested script is: 'Hey. I love our dates together and want to keep spending time with you. I'm on a budget right now, so I can *(INSERT YOUR DATE SUGGESTIONS/FREQUENCY HERE)*.'

- **Set a budget.** Calculate how much you can afford to spend on dates each month. Put the money aside in a designated online pot or on a dedicated card. This will stop you from overspending on your dates. But it will also protect your all-important fun money from being eaten into by daily expenses.

- **Be proactive.** You mention that your boo and your friends are arranging dates that are out of your budget. This is almost definitely not on purpose; they just don't have a good idea of your budget. If you plan the dates and issue the invites, then you can make sure that the activity is within your spending allowance.

THE THIRD LOVE LANGUAGE

ACTS OF SERVICE

Does the idea of a dark, dangerous-looking stranger offering to carry your bag send you weak at the knees? Or are you in desperate need of advice because your SO never notices when you need help and it's driving you batty?

People who value acts of service see actions as an expression of affection. Picture the pointy-toothed smile on your boo's face when someone surprises them with a quick bite.

This chapter has all the info you need – we're going to (grave) dig into the meaning of acts of service, learn how to keep things balanced and take a look at self-care – **or should we say self-service?**

Here are four guidelines for how to warm the cold, undead heart of your crush if you think their love language is acts of service:

Be proactive. Don't wait to be asked for assistance. Look out for ways you can help and make the offer.

Details. They say the devil is in the detail, but guess what? So is the vampire. Notice the little things that stress your crush, not just the big things, and help out where you can.

Find balance. There will be things that you are better at than your crush – such as being out in broad daylight. Help your boo do the things they aren't strong at and together you can be the sun and the moon, both shining in different situations.

Don't overpromise . . . and then underdeliver. A broken promise hurts like a silver cross to an acts-of-service crush. Only say you will do the things you know you have the time to do. Hotties who value acts of service are straightforward and they would rather you were honest about not being able to do something than be let down after you made a promise.

HOW DO YOU KNOW IF YOUR LOVE LANGUAGE IS ACTS OF SERVICE?

I'm a straight-shooting agony aunt and I stake from the hip. *Look*, you might be thinking, *doesn't everyone like it when someone does something nice for them? Is acts of service my love language, or does it just feel good when someone makes my life a little easier?*

To that, I say, let's investigate! If acts of service is your way of expressing your affection, you may already be speaking that love language without realising it.

Let's look at some actions that you may take if your love language is acts of service:

- **You know what's going on with people.** You not only hear people when they say they have a big deadline or keep forgetting to make an important appointment, but you actively think of ways to help.

- **Their mission is your mission.** You're always internet sleuthing to find that one cute necklace that your good sis thought was sold out everywhere or whisking up a home remedy because your bestie mentioned they were under the weather.

- **You get it right *a lot* of the time.** You don't just pick a brunch spot; you pick a place that suits everyone's dietary requirements and has more than one option for the picky eater. That's because you pay attention.

- **In your opinion, the best weapons in your arsenal are time and effort.** You'll plot, plan, scheme, tinker, make and craft your way to make your loved ones happy.

Essentially, **you're an action-focused person.** You may not always have the right words on the tip of your tongue, but you are always the first person to say 'I'll do it' when someone asks for a favour.

Learning another love language

If acts of service doesn't sound like your love language, don't fret. Here come Crimson's translation services, ready to help you learn. But how can you speak a language that doesn't use words? Well, with my help, you'll know just what to do – and by doing, you'll be saying.

- **Set reminders and plan accordingly.** What, you thought organisation wasn't swoon-worthy? Well, for some, colour-coded calendars are their own love language. You'll be using these reminders to recall the big events and stress points in your boo's life and plot some kind actions around these times. Whether it's bringing them a surprise takeaway drink on a difficult day or taking a chore off their hands around a big deadline, you'll be surprised how these little efforts count as big gestures for your SO.

- **There's no job too boring.** You may wonder if helping them change their bicycle chain is going to really make their knees weak. *Yes, it is!*

- **Remember, it's acts of service, not acts of surprise.** If you feel your favours have been falling flat with your boo, ask what they'd like you to do for them. For example, it may be that you've been focused on solving their problems when actually they're more interested in having their mind taken off their stresses.

Like a stake through the heart

For every act of service that makes your boo swoon, there's a series of actions that drive deeper than a stake. I call these a hate language. Just like learning your boo's love language is a great way to find harmony in your relationship, learning your crush's hate language helps you avoid arguments and conflict.

Here are some of the things that make up the hate language for someone who speaks acts of service.

Am I a ghost?

Acts of service can be small and practical, and therefore less showy than generous gifts or flowery language. But less showy shouldn't mean invisible. Remember to say thank you and show your appreciation for these kind gestures. Otherwise, your boo might start to wonder, can anyone see me? Am I a ghost?

Compelled to act

Your boo may show their love through acts of service but that doesn't give you free rein to use compulsion on them and start handing out chore lists for them to complete. Your affection should be given freely and not won through endless quests. Remember, the vibe is badass in the moonlight, not princess in the castle.

Telepathy fail

Readers with super-sight will notice a bit of a theme in all of these chapters. *Crimson*, you say, *you don't stop droning on about how telepathy and compulsion don't work*. And guess what! I'm going to do it again. If you have a task or a problem you'd like your acts-of-service-seeking boo to help you with, you have to tell them! If you don't, you run the risk of being disappointed when they don't read your mind.

MY KIND OF ACT

The writing is on the tarot cards – your ultimate love language is acts of service. But everyone wants help with different things.

Take this quiz to figure out what kind of acts of service suit you best.

Your boo is down in the dumps. Their evil twin has stolen their beloved family heirloom. Sure, there are hundreds of the things, but this one really meant something to them! Do you:

A: Scour the web – and a few underground witch shops – until you find them a replacement. That heirloom can't be the only one of its kind.

B: Study pictures of the heirloom and use your crafting skills to make a version of it to gift to your boo.

C: Run interference. You won't commit a crime, but if your boo needs you to distract the evil twin while they get the heirloom back, you're in.

D: Plan a cute date and help them take their mind off things. It's time for Operation Cheer Up Boo!

You're going to a wedding together and your boo is worried they'll stick out – it's been decades since they last attended one. Do you:

A: Create a compilation of the wedding scenes from your favourite movies and TV shows. At least they'll be surprised when no one objects during the ceremony.

B: Gather all the details you can from the invite, the wedding website and any inside gossip you can (without harassing the bride and groom). Create your own 'what's on' for the day, including any tips and tricks your boo will find useful.

C: Spend your spare weekends teaching them a few dance moves. They will find it tricky to waltz to Taylor Swift.

D: Tell them that if they do something strange, you'll copy it. You can be glorious weirdos together.

Your boo comes to you with a dilemma: they think they've been cursed by a witch. Do you:

A: Contact the best witches in the area. They'll have the curse lifted in no time.

B: Research curse breaking. Every curse can be broken, you just need to find the solution.

C: Help your boo plot their countermove. No one does this to your crush and gets away with it!

D: Make them a 'sorry you've been cursed' care package with all their favourite goodies.

There appears to be a secret society operating on campus and your SO is on to them. But they seem to be on to your SO as well! Do you:

A: Take to the archives – there must be some clues on how to bring about their downfall embedded in the ancient text section.

B: Gift your SO some crystals that may or may not be blessed by a local witch with protective wards. No one is going to harm them on your watch.

C: Launch a take-over of the secret society. No one is kicking out your boo now you're the president.

D: Make a kickass playlist to accompany their research. It's time for a montage . . .

Yes! Your crush's favourite musician is coming to town. Do you:

A: Forward them the news, along with gig times, links to the support act's music and transport times. They're going to be so happy to hear this.

B: Craft a DIY merch tee to wear to the gig. A unique bit of merch, just for them.

C: Buy tickets for you both to attend. Simple.

D: Contact the musician ahead of the gig to ask them to give your boo a shout-out. You know that will make their experience even more special.

RESULTS

Mostly As: You're into practical magic. You're a whizz – or should that be witch – with researching, planning and – when necessary – outsourcing.

Mostly Bs: You're a creative – a true shapeshifter. You like to make and craft your way to making your loved one's day.

Mostly Cs: You're action-focused, the quintessential pack-mate. You'll go the extra mile, literally running it if need be, if it will help the one you love.

Mostly Ds: You're an empath. You're in tune with how your boo is feeling and your acts of service are all designed to keep your crush feeling light, lifted and supported.

Make your crush blush

Acts of service boos have super-enhanced hearing. They don't just hear what you say; they can also pick up on the secret messages that you're broadcasting. They read between the lines and notice what you might need, want or enjoy. If you are new to the language of service, here are some examples of what your boo might say and how you might react:

💜 *I'm so busy balancing work and my hobbies on X day, I always end up being in a rush to have lunch.*

   Act of service: Pack your crush a snack that's easily consumed on the go.

💜 *This is my favourite brand of lip balm, but they're always sold out at my local shop.*

   Act of service: Stay on the lookout for places where the lip balm is always in stock and tell your boo or buy them some next time you see it.

💜 *I love listening to music when I exercise!*

   Act of service: Create a playlist that you think will get your boo's adrenaline pumping and share it with them.

Dating disaster

You've had the best day with your boo. You went shopping and they opened all the doors for you and used their super-strength to carry your bags when they got too heavy. You grabbed food at your favourite street-food stall and when they saw how long the queue was they offered to order for you both while you sat down. Lunch was amazing, as usual, and the company was perfection.

However, after lunch your boo appeared down. Clouds drifted over the sky and into their face. A storm opened up above their head. You took the hint and asked what was wrong. They said that you never notice the things they do for you. Erm, not true! You love that they are kind and thoughtful. But you thought that's just how they are – are you expected to say thank you every time? How will you manage to maintain any conversations if all you do is say 'thank you, thank you'?

Showing appreciation

You shouldn't stop saying thank you and being grateful just because being kind and generous is in your SO's nature. You may stop being surprised that your boo performs acts of service for you but that doesn't mean you should stop being grateful. The gestures may be small and happen a lot but they're still your boo's way of saying they think you're the coolest.

You are right that making a big deal out of every gesture might be overkill and not your boo's style, but there are lots of ways to show your appreciation that fit seamlessly in with your everyday interactions.

Appreciating the little things. No gesture, no matter how small, should go unnoticed. A quick thanks in the moment goes a long way.

Here are some things you can do:

✦ **Tell your boo the impact their actions had on you.** Calling out the way you benefited from their kind gesture – saying something like 'thank you for chasing off those werewolves the other day, they really helped me get more work done' – can make them feel seen.

✦ **Be approving.** If your boo put a lot of work into picking a brunch place that is a hit, be vocal about it. Tell them what you like – the décor, the menu, the music, the zombie-free location – and they'll know their effort was worth it.

✦ **Write a gratitude list.** If you feel like you're starting to let your boo's small-but-wonderful acts of service slip off the radar, spend some time at the end of the day writing a gratitude list. This should include all the things they did for you that day. Giving their kindness some focused attention will help you start to notice the small things again.

Dear Crimson,

I love helping out! If there's a curse to break, I'm on it. Secret sigils inscribed around campus? I'll investigate! A friend on their holidays? I'll feed their bloodhound. I love the feeling of being useful to my besties. But I'm starting to feel as though people only want to spend time with me when they have a problem. I like helping people, but I don't want to be riding to the rescue all the time. Am I doomed to always miss the party and get invited to the clean-up?

Saviour Complex

Hey, Saviour

It sounds like your love language is acts of service. You've found a way to show your affection but now you're stuck riding to the rescue. Honestly, you save the world one or five times and suddenly all your invites are to apocalypses. Would it kill someone to invite you to brunch?!

Firstly, let's break the habit of only lending a helping hand in a crisis. Let's switch your mindset from noticing the negatives to celebrating the positives. Here is a quick list of fun, positive acts of service you could try instead:

- Slip cute notes in their bag.
- Create playlists.
- If you have an artistic or crafty skill, use it to make something. Why not whittle them a protection talisman?
- Support your friend at their underground gig or super-strength baseball match.

Secondly, you sound worried that you are being taken for granted or seen as more of a helper than a friend. One thing you could do here is to take the initiative and organise a couple of hangouts yourself. What would you like to do with your friends? Pick a couple of possible dates and invite them to do that.

Another solution is one that I always recommend. Talk directly to your friends about your worries. Next time they ask you for a favour tell them that you can't help out at the moment, but you'd be up for hanging out if they're free and suggest something fun to do together like snake charming.

Always here to serve,
Crimson

Don't be a Compelled...

Life in the twilight can be a lonely one, whether you're a genius scientist harnessing the power of life and death or a good-looking vampire just looking for somewhere to spend eternity. Legend says that a mysterious and powerful figure who lives in a castle must be in want of a spooky assistant.

Although these figures seem to have it all – immense intelligence, unfathomable wealth, a home conveniently located in a lightning-storm hot spot – they still need help.

Dark-sided vampires use their Compelled to run errands, do favours and make their lives easier. No sooner has a Compelled completed a task than they receive another one.

Good friends and boos will never take advantage of someone like that. But you may occasionally encounter a Big Bad who wants to twist your love language to their own advantage.

Here are a few red flags that suggest your crush may be entering their villain era:

- **Annoying tasks get assigned to you**, instead of being shared out between you and your boo, or the slay squad.

- **You find yourself being 'voluntold' to do things,** with phrases like 'you'll do that, won't you?'

- **Your boo gets annoyed with you for not doing them certain favours** – but they never asked you to do them in the first place.

- **'Thank you' seems to drop out of their vocabulary** and you feel taken for granted.

- **Your acts of service are dismissed or diminished** as something you 'should' do rather than something you choose to do.

Energy vampires

Some vampires aren't bloodsuckers. They feed on your energy instead. These are known as energy vampires or psychic vampires. Unlike standard vampires, which can come in every flavour from friendly neighbourhood vamp to evil and ancient, energy vampires are nearly always toxic presences.

Like standard vampires, they often hide their vampiric nature from you to start with. However, you were quick to cotton on to the fact your newest crush wasn't entirely human. After all, who uses that much sun cream on a cloudy day? With energy vampires, the signs are harder to spot. They can't get past Crimson Angel Mercy, though!

Here is my field guide to spotting an energy vampire in the wild . . .

- **They transform your good news into their misfortune.** You tell them that you got a PB on your latest run. They congratulate you, but quickly switch the conversation to their challenges finding a good place to run, their dislike of their local running club, and on and on and on.

- **You tell them that your crush asked you out on a date.** They share that they're worried they will never find anyone. No matter how amazing your news is, they quickly change the subject to their own concerns.

- **They always need help from you but have no time for your problems.** You bring up something that's upset you – perhaps your boo has started acting strangely since their probably evil twin arrived in town – hoping to talk through your feelings. However, the conversation quickly gets turned back to their worries and fears.

- **They take advantage of your love language.** They use your love of helping others to always ask for favours, and the favours keep getting bigger. Or they've worked out that you're a gift giver and ask you to buy them things (more on this in chapter five).

- **They are masters of the guilt trip.** Just when you finally decide to break the habit and establish a boundary with them, they start the guilt trip. You might say that your budget means you can't pay for their share of the bill any more. They reply that they knew that you never really liked them.

- **They don't really want a win.** Most people don't want to be stuck in their rough patch. They want to be happy and healthy, moving onwards and upwards. But energy vampires know that once they're in a good place, the sympathy and support that feeds them will dry up. You may notice that although they're happy to talk about their problems, they're not interested in discussing solutions.

Be self-serving

Even bloodsucking baddies need a self-care routine. And so do their love interests. You may find that you feel drained – but happy – after a successful day of wooing and boo-ing. Planning and executing acts of service can be tiring. After all, you are sending your good vibes out into the world with the intention of making it a better place.

Reserve some of your time and energy for giving yourself the kindness that you are so willing to share with others. After all, you deserve all the feelings of being loved and understood that you give out with your acts of service. Ask yourself, *What would I do for my boo if they were in my situation?* And then, do it!

If you are still struggling to get into the self-serving mindset, then turn the page for a handful of quick and easy acts of self-service.

💜 **Pick up a pampering treat**, such as a sheet mask or bath oil. Pick a fragrance that has dark, vampiric notes, such as rose, frankincense and wood. Light some candles and have a quiet, mystic evening.

💜 **Watch your favourite episodes of your comfort series.** Wouldn't it be nice of someone to plan a low-key evening spent with all your favourite characters – make that person you!

💜 **Switch off socials.** Have you heard of doom scrolling? It's where you scroll socials and other sites, seemingly with no purpose, feeding negative thoughts. Turn off your socials and unplug for the evening.

💜 **Write positive affirmations** on a piece of paper and stick them by your mirror. Perhaps something like, 'I am stronger, I am powerful, I have yet to be cursed.' You will read those messages every time you look in the mirror and feel a burst of positivity.

More than I bargained for!

Dear Crimson,

A bad vamp with a sweet side rolled into town and we've been hanging out. We're not even at the talking stage, but to be honest, I kind of like them. They're always doing the nicest things for me – they pick me up bubble teas and they super-sped back to the park to pick up the blanket I forgot. They always lend me their coat when I get cold because they don't ever feel the cold!

Except . . . Now they're saying I have to go on a date with them because they did all those great things for me. They say that I owe them my time and if I don't go, it will mean I'm a user who manipulated them. Crimson, I'm not a user! I thought they were just being kind because that's who they were – I didn't realise that I was manipulating them into doing me favours. I feel so bad.

I probably would have gone on a date with them before they said all this. But I don't like how they went about it. So . . . should I just go?

Yours,
They Burst My Bubble Tea

Dear Bubble,

Oh dear. I've got to break it to you: you haven't been hanging out with a vampire. They aren't even a dhampir – a half vampire, half human. They're an imp. And not any old imp – a Rumpelstiltskin!

I do have some good news for you. You're not a user and you are not manipulative. This Rumpelstiltskin has tried to lay a trap for you. They've given you a gift – whether that's a treat, or their time and effort – waited for you to accept it and then told you there are strings attached to it.

You didn't know, and you didn't agree to those conditions. How dare they try to trick you like that? It's time to get all medieval fairy tale on their butt. We're talking learning their true name, finding their hidden artefacts, creating mirror traps and setting impossible riddles that they have to solve.

Now you know that future favours aren't really favours at all, they're traps, and you can turn them

down. Sure, you might enjoy fewer free bubble teas, but at least you won't be tricked by false friends. As for Rumpel, I suggest replying to him with one of three responses:

If he brings up his past favours: Thank you.

If he asks you on a date: I don't want to go on a date with you.

If he tries to do something new for you: No, thank you.

Always here to serve,
Crimson

Bloodsucker moment

Someone's done something nice for me but I didn't want them to, and now they're saying I have to do x, y and z.

This is sometimes called favour-sharking, a term based on loan sharks. Loan sharks lend people sums of money at a high interest rate, which means they have to pay back lots more money than they borrowed. Here in the supernatural and mythological beings community, we call those guys Rumpelstiltskins. Rumpelstiltskins will do something nice for you – maybe even something you need. But it always comes with a catch. Wait! Are you thinking this sounds like the cutie you've been pining after? They also like to do you favours or help you out with things.

There's one crucial difference to look out for. People who love to offer their acts of service don't expect anything in return. Rumpelstiltskins always ask for something in return. They might get you something thoughtful, like a baked treat from a bakery you once mentioned. But then they pressure you to buy them lunch, because you 'owe' them.

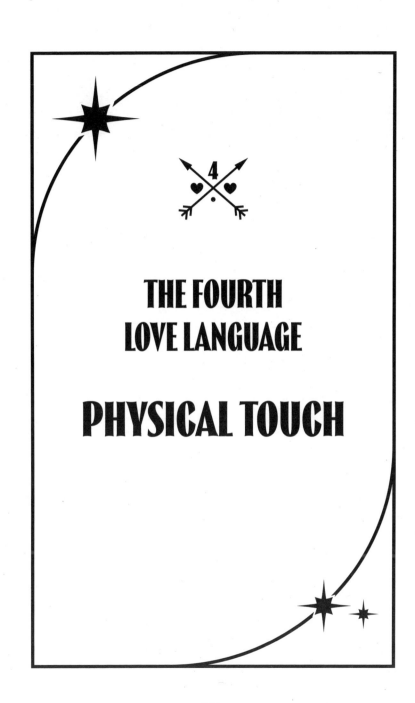

THE FOURTH
LOVE LANGUAGE

PHYSICAL TOUCH

Does your heart beat faster when your boo puts their arm around you? Are you unsure about your boundaries and how to communicate them? Are you ready to go in for the kiss but not sure if your partner wants that too? Don't worry, Crimson's got you. I'm going to give you my guide to getting romantic, discussing boundaries, spotting red flags and staying true to yourself.

Practising physical touch is about showing your SO that you are there for them and providing physical demonstrations of your affection. It's one of the most romantic love languages, and also one of the most sincere. After all, words can have double and triple meanings but a hug is much simpler.

Be physically present. Make a point to sit next to them when you're in a group, or plan an evening just curled up on the sofa together.

Big gestures. Show your support for your partner through their highs and lows with physical contact such as shoulder rubs and firm hugs.

Little touches. Small physical gestures provide your boo with little touchpoints throughout the day, such as touching their arm as you pass or brushing their hair out of their eyes.

Body language. Your SO will be very attuned to the message your body sends. You can send them positive vibes by making lots of eye contact, pointing your body towards them while you talk and appearing engaged and invested.

PDA. Don't try to hide the affection between the two of you. Physical-touch crushes love to hold hands or walk with their arms around each other in public.

HOW DO YOU KNOW IF YOUR LOVE LANGUAGE IS PHYSICAL TOUCH?

The signs that your love language is physical touch will be there, even before you have your first relationship. After all, people who speak in physical touch are expressive – you guys wear your hearts on your sleeves.

Are you known in your friendship group as the hugger? Do you ever finish telling a story and discover that you've got your listener's hand in yours? The clues are all there!

How about these actions? If you do these, there's a good chance you're all about physical touch.

· **You talk with your hands.** Your hands are as busy as your mouth when you are deep in conversation, always emphasising your point by clasping your friend's arm, clapping them on the back and taking them by the hand.

· **You're a big believer in 'hugging it out'** after a disagreement with a loved one. There's something about a hug that feels almost like a physical reconnection after an argument.

· **Your personal space bubble is a lot smaller than other people's**, especially when spending time with someone you like. In fact, you prefer to sit closely to someone and you don't mind if your legs overlap or you have to tuck one arm under another.

· **You are very sensitive to body language.** You struggle to connect with people who look disinterested, hold themselves defensively with crossed arms, or who angle their body away from you. To you, they're broadcasting that they aren't interested.

If you are extra sensitive to the natural dopamine hit that comes with interactions such as hugs and hand holding, then your love language may be physical touch.

Learning another love language

Have you developed a crush on a hottie who is all about physical touch? Do you want to show them that you care in their favourite love language, but you're unsure how to go about that? Perhaps you're interested in being physically affectionate but you don't come from a very huggy family. Maybe physical touch just isn't your first love language. Thankfully I have just the thing you need.

Here's my guide to speaking your SO's love language:

- **Hold their hand or put your arm around them when you're on the go.** This is a way to communicate that you're here with them and you're proud to be seen with them, without ever having to say a word.

- **Soft touches demonstrate the tender feelings you share.** If you're both comfortable with it, romantic gestures like playing with your boo's supernaturally perfect hair or running your fingers along their wrists or neck work well.

- **Physical comfort means the most to your SO.** They don't need long flowery speeches when they're feeling down. If they come to you with a problem, they may not be looking for you to help them solve it. Instead, they'd love you to hold them in your arms, perhaps stroke their back or play with their hair. Just be physically present for them.

ALL YOU Need is love

Like a stake through the heart

Low-contact love affairs

Hotties who speak in physical touch thrive off the presence of their boo. When they don't see their crush for a long time – and therefore miss out on all the gestures of affection that tell them they are cared for – they feel insecure in the relationship. Whether their partner got busy feuding with local werewolves or got sent to a boarding school for supernatural elites, messages, video calls and the occasional handwritten letter sealed with wax just isn't enough to keep the fires burning.

Giving the cold shoulder

Being undead, all vampires' shoulders are cold. But when they give the cold shoulder, it involves avoiding their boo, not answering messages and being physically separate from them if they are in the same space. It's the physical separation that particularly hurts them. To them, it feels as though cold water is being poured over their feelings.

Sneaky links

Being someone's sneaky link – a relationship that is kept on the downlow – isn't for everyone. It really hurts those who crave physical touch. Vampires may do well in the darkness but that doesn't mean they want their relationship to be kept in the shadows. They like their partners to state publicly, through hand holding, hugs and other gestures, that they are together and proud of it.

THE MYSTERY ARRIVAL

Uh-oh, your crush has been acting shady. They've started avoiding you and you've caught sight of them with another person.

You do some digging and discover a member of their extensive, and frankly weird, family has popped up in town.

But which one?

You can't judge a book by its cover, but you can almost certainly judge a vamp by their outfit. This mysterious stranger is wearing:

A: Lots of leather jewellery and very tight trousers. They look a little bit like a rockstar.

B: A sharp suit, straight off the red carpet. And wow, their hair is immaculate. Does it even stir in the breeze?

C: Very similar clothes to your boo. But with more leather.

D: An unassuming outfit. You almost suspect they're trying not to stand out.

There have been reports of mysterious activity in the town, starting just before they arrived. You've heard:

A: That lots of valuables have gone missing.

B: That the town's mayor has started making strange, out-of-character decisions. Almost like they're being told what to do.

C: That your crush has been acting very strangely. They've been so mean to people they're usually nice to.

D: That people have been asking around town whether anyone has seen someone who matched the newcomer's description.

You've had enough of the mystery. You ask your boo who this new person is and they tell you:

A: To stay away from them.

B: To stay away from them.

C: To stay away from them.

D: To stay away from them.

Vampires always say the same thing when it comes to mysterious newcomers. One day, in the local coffee shop, you bump into the stranger. They:

A: Say something that sounds poetic but actually makes no sense when you think about it.

B: Warn you to stay away from your partner.

C: Pretend they're your boo, even though you completely see through them.

D: Seem really friendly. You don't know why your SO was so worried about you meeting them. Perhaps they have access to baby photos?

RESULTS

Mostly As: The wild one. You're not sure if this family member is a hero or a villain and you don't think they know either. Either way, life is never boring when they come to town. Honestly? If this was *Vampire Diaries*, they'd be Klaus.

Mostly Bs: The authoritarian figure – the Elijah. They just want the best for your boo, but that doesn't necessarily involve you. They want everyone to play by their rules.

Mostly Cs: The evil twin. They bring chaos whenever they visit. You find yourself gritting your teeth and putting up with them for your boo's sake. A subsection of the evil twin is the evil sibling, of which Damon Salvatore is the perfect example.

Mostly Ds: The little sibling with a secret. They are always so nice to you, but they come with a lot of baggage – hello, Rebekah. You're pretty sure a rescue mission will be involved whenever they visit.

This or that: Romance edition

Do you dare take my romance edition of this or that with the ghoulfriends? This is for all those who go weak at the knees and the heart at physical touch.

Which little romantic gestures make your stomach flip-flop, and which ones give you the ick?

Brushing hands as you both reach for something or knees pressing together under the table?

Super-speeding with you in their arms or super-strength jumping with you on their back?

Holding hands as you walk down the road or putting their arm around your shoulders when you sit down?

Slow dancing at a ball or rocking out at a nightclub?

Kissing your temple or nuzzling your neck?

Tucking your hair behind your ear or brushing an eyelash off your cheek?

First kiss in the rain or first kiss after defeating henchmen?

An evening cuddling on the sofa with a film or an afternoon lounging in the grass with a picnic?

Dear Crimson,

I have a serious dilemma. I've been seeing a cute vampire for a little while now and it's going very well. They are amazing - I'm blushing and clicking my heels so much that I've developed a light heat rash and RSI. There is one small hitch. They are a bad kisser. I'm talking a mouth pursed like a black cat's butthole, a tongue that revolves like a washing machine and worst of all - fangs. I come away from every kiss with a wet face and cut lips. My dream date is turning into a nightmare.

I've been dropping some pretty heavy hints. I've even sent them video compilations of my favourite on-screen kisses. Help me, Crimson, I've run out of ways to subtly towel myself dry after a make-out session.

No Love Bites Please

Hey, Love Bite,

You know, as a part-time agony aunt, part-time vamp buster and full-time badass, I've seen it all. The washing machine tongue. The Grand Canyon mouth. The garlic breath (this is a real problem in the vampire dating community).

For something so natural, kissing is surprisingly hard to master. My theory is that we all like different things, so what feels like being smooched by Casanova himself to some people will be more like being mauled by a mangy werewolf to others.

I like your thinking with the compilation of hottest kisses. But I have to tell you: a hint, however heavy, is unlikely to do the trick. You're going to have to be honest with your SO. This is a case where it's possible to be too honest. I would leave out any descriptive words and certainly any mention of a black cat's butthole. Instead, frame your feedback positively.

Don't just tell them what you don't like; think about what you do like and share that with them instead:

'I'm more into soft kisses.'

'I like it when you kiss me slowly but deeply.'

'I enjoy kisses on my jaw or my neck – can you spend some time doing that too?'

If all else fails, may I recommend microfibre towels? They are very absorbent and fold small enough to fit in a pocket or bag, so they can always be on hand.

Always here to serve,
Crimson

YES, NO AND MAYBE

If you've found your partner, you may be interested in expressing your feelings for them through physical intimacy, such as kissing. This is where you must master the mystic art of communication, in order to clearly tell your boo what you want to do and learn what they want to do. You can't assume that just because you feel ready to take the next step, your partner does too. And they should never assume that because they're interested in exploring a new physical touch, you are too.

I get asked about this all the time, and everyone – from teen wolves to original vampires – can do with some help getting it right. Let's talk it through:

> When is the right time to introduce a new physical touch, like holding hands, to my relationship with my boo?

> The right time is when you both want to introduce a new physical touch.

How will I know when the other person wants to hold hands with me?

You can ask them if they'd like to hold hands.

That sounds embarrassing! How would I ask without sounding really old-fashioned and boring?

Keep it clear, simple and sweet. Make sure you name the action that you'd like to do clearly, to avoid confusion.

OK! So, I could say, 'I'd like to hold hands with you.'

That isn't a question.

Saying something like, 'I'd like to hold hands with you' or 'I want to kiss you now' tells the other person what you are interested in doing, but doesn't give them the chance to say yes or no or tell you what they want.

Make sure you phrase your request as a question.

How about, 'Would you like to hold hands?'

Perfect. You could also say 'May I hold your hand?' or add a question to a statement, such as, 'I want to hold your hand. Would you like to?'

They didn't say yes, but they also didn't say no! Shall I count that as a yes?

The only thing that counts as a yes is a yes. No, silence or a 'yes, but' should be taken as a no from your boo.

Wait, that's confusing! You're telling me that my boo might say something that sounds like a yes but means no. How can I tell?

You should listen for verbal clues. An enthusiastic yes won't be followed by a contradictory word. These words include 'but', 'although' and 'wait'. Other phrases that are code for no include 'not right now', 'maybe' or 'I'm not sure'.

You should also watch for visual clues. Crossed arms, chest pointed away and downcast eyes all point to someone who is not feeling confident in the conversation.

Bloodsucker moment

There's a classic dilemma that can occur when you develop a crush on someone. You like their style, you share their interests, you admire their personality. But wait . . . do you want to be *with* them or do you want to *be* them? This kind of crush – the kind where you really admire someone but aren't actually attracted to them – is known as an identity crush.

Identity crushes are very common, especially when you first start falling for people. How can you tell the difference between an identity crush and a romantic crush?

Here are some signs you've developed an identity crush:

❤ **You put your crush on a pedestal.** We all view our crushes with rose-tinted glasses, but when you have an identity crush, you really can't see their flaws. Perhaps you think they're not the sort of person to have flaws, but everyone – vampires and humans alike – has flaws.

❤ **You look up to your crush.** It's common to think of your crush as incredibly cool, but you usually still think of them as on your level. This is known as your peer. When you have an identity crush, you feel as though your crush is above you or ahead of you in some way.

❤ **You want to copy your crush.** Perhaps they've nailed their sense of fashion and you wish you looked more like them. Maybe their taste in music is amazing and you wish you could lift their playlists. Perhaps their comic timing is impeccable and you fantasise about being able to make people laugh like they do. Unlike with a romantic crush, where you are attracted to the things you have in common, with an identity crush you're attracted to the attributes you wish you had.

❤ **An identity crush is really, really intense.** It's mixed up with your own sense of identity and that adds an extra level of feeling.

Can an identity crush turn into a relationship? In my experience, it usually doesn't. It's tough to start a relationship when you feel like your boo is way above you. The good news is that once the intensity of an identity crush has faded, you don't usually have lingering romantic feelings.

Squish crush

A squish crush is another name for a friend crush. A friend crush is when you fall for someone, but as a best friend. You meet them and you basically know that this is your person – but platonically. What are the signs that you've developed a friend crush rather than a romantic crush?

Here are a few of the hallmarks:

- **You are OBSESSED with each other.** There aren't enough hours in the day to spend time together, and when you're not physically together, you're snapping and messaging each other non-stop.

- **You feel a zing of excitement** ahead of your meetups or a little thrill when you see a notification from your bestie.

- **You are a fan of your bestie, but you're also such a stan of your friendship couple.** You bring out the best in each other, and as far as you're concerned, no one is doing it like you two.

- **It's all the rush, but none of the blush?** You feel all these amazing endorphins when you spend time with your squish crush, but you don't feel that spark of attraction that makes you blush.

It may feel confusing when you first develop a squish crush because your feelings are so intense. However, once you realise your emotions towards your friend are platonic, you can sit back and simply enjoy being part of an amazing double act.

The great disappearing crush

Dear Crimson,

Recently I've grown closer to my crush. We seem to bump into each other all the time, and we've started to hang out more. At first, I had butterflies in my stomach every time I saw them! Our hands would brush together and I'd be blushing, giggling and kicking my feet. I haven't felt butterflies in a while, though. The other day their hand touched mine and I didn't feel a thing. Where did the spark go? I thought they were going to be The One.

Fickle Fiend

Hey, Fiend,

Doctor Crimson here. My diagnosis is that you've come down with a terrible case of . . . a completely normal crush. Some crushes blossom into love, some fizzle into friendship, some even turn into dislike!

Sometimes people start as friends and develop a crush. Some of the greatest love stories start with two people completely hating each other and then developing a crush. Some vampires live for so long that they start with a crush, become enemies, go back to being friends, develop a crush, fall in love and end up as enemies again. Exhausting! And much more fun to read about than to experience.

It sounds as though you had a crush that fizzled. Physical touch is a great way to test whether the spark is there – when you are attracted to someone, something small like a brush of a hand can feel very exciting. When you feel only friendship or less, a hand feels just like a hand.

The next stages are up to you. From what you said in your letter, there's potential for friendship here. You seem to be getting on well. But if you're no longer interested in getting to know your former crush now that the feelings have faded, then you don't need to. Be sure to let them down gently and don't ghost them.

Always here to serve,
Crimson

Calculate your ship name

Wise relationship counsellors (wait, that's me) say that the best way to succeed as a couple is to act as a team. And not only act as a team but be your own team supporters. Even better, support yourselves like you were your endgame couple in your favourite show. After all, who goes harder in the name of love than the stans of certain ships? Stans can back couples that have only ever exchanged three words. They are ride or die for two people who have never even met. That's the energy you need to harness! Every time you struggle to compromise or get stuck on an argument, think to yourself, how would I make this relationship work if I were a stan?

The first step to shipping yourself is generating your couple name. Are you going to name-smoosh? Codename?

Check out my ship-name generator and find the right one for you.

How to create your ship name:

Slash. The easiest way to create a ship name is to insert a forward slash between your two names. This creates a simple ship name, such as You/Boo. It's elegant. Timeless. Just like a vampire.

Smoosh name. Also known as a portmanteau. You take half of your name and half of your partner's name and make a new name. For example, Crimson Angel Mercy + Vampire Boo might create the ship name CrimPire. Hmm, that doesn't have the romantic ring I was hoping for.

Personal qualities. Instead of combining your names, you could combine certain attributes. Vampires turn into bats, you're a human; you could combine the two words and get the ship name Batman. No, wait, I think that's taken. . .

Significant moments. Name your ship after somewhere or something that has romantic importance to your relationship. For example, if one of your date rituals is to visit the record shop on New Music Fridays, your fans (yourself) might engage in VinylShipping.

THE FIFTH
LOVE LANGUAGE

GIFT GIVING AND
RECEIVING

Do your knees go weak when your partner returns from the shops with a little treat for you in their bag? Or do you feel the pressure of giving the perfect deathday present because you know how much it means to your SO?

Gift giving and receiving is easily one of the most misunderstood love languages. People who don't have a kickass love language and supernatural entity expert (moi) to explain things to them may think gift receivers are materialistic. I know better.

Gift givers and receivers are similar to physical touch givers and receivers. They value expressions of love that they can see and touch. Inexpert eyes might simply see a material possession, but gift givers see a physical representation of the thought and affection that went into selecting the present.

Personal. Valued gifts are very personal to the person receiving them. Whether you base your gift on a reference to something the recipient said in passing or something that has been on their wish list for years, it really is the thought that counts.

Special occasions. Recognise that special occasions such as birthdays or holidays should always include a thoughtful gift. Plan well ahead of the date in order to factor in delivery times.

Regular occurrences. You don't have to wait for a special occasion to give a thoughtful gift. Keep an eye out for opportunities to give your boo a small but thoughtful present. Bring snacks to theirs on movie nights, return from holidays with gifts and or pick up little presents while you're out 'just because'.

Get creative. Your gifts don't have to cost the earth. Those blessed with generosity appreciate the thought that has gone into baking homemade treats or crafting a handmade present.

HOW DO YOU KNOW IF YOUR LOVE LANGUAGE IS GIFT GIVING AND RECEIVING?

Do you get weirdly excited around other people's birthdays? You may not be the one receiving the gifts but you're still buzzing. You can't wait until they open the present and you see their reaction. They've been dying to refresh their collection of ancient relics for so long. In your mind, gifts are tangible proof of the time you spend thinking about another person. If this sounds like you, then you might be a gift giver and receiver.

If you're still not sure, here are some other signs to help clue you in:

- **Nothing gets past you!** You remember even the smallest passing comment and will use the info to help you curate the perfect gift.

- **Your besties are always on your mind.** It's almost as though you see the world through their eyes as well as yours. Wherever you go, you see things that your bestie would love or your boo would go wild for.

- **You are a little bit of a hoarder.** You find it really hard to throw away old cards or pass on items that were gifted. To you, everything has a story. Your friends know if they compliment one of your possessions, then they are about to hear its entire life story.

- **You are known as the generous one in the group.** As far as you're concerned, sharing is caring.

- **You have a little bit of an overspending problem** that usually strikes around the holidays. You can't help it if you have a vision that you need to execute.

If you're kind, generous and feel a deep emotional connection to tangible objects, then gift giving and receiving may just be your love language.

Learning another love language

Are you a chronically bad gift giver? Do you feel as though someone has cast a spell to blank your mind every time you attempt to shop for other people's birthdays? All this talk of the gift-giving love language is making you nervous. Especially if your vampire boo is able to pull the most amazing antiques from their archives, while you're getting them a voucher for Coffins4U online.

Never fear, Crimson is here! Let's look at the secrets of taking your gifting technique from underwhelming to fang-tastic . . .

- **Think personalised gifts.** Does that advice get your pulse racing with panic, wondering what personal means? I'm talking gifts that relate to your boo's hobbies, interests, dreams, even their past. Forget generic gifts such as vouchers, unless your boo specifically requests them.

- **Keep a list of ideas and references** as you think of them. Don't wait until two weeks before the gift-giving date to start thinking about it, or you'll have to rack your brain and pay massive shipping fees for last-minute deliveries.

- **Think outside the box** – and don't limit yourself to only gifting on special occasions. Pick up a little gift when you're on holiday or even on a day trip to tell your boo, 'Hey, I was away but still thinking of you.' You could also bring edible treats to your hangouts.

- **Turn generic gifts into genres.** Hotties who value gift giving and receiving are all about personalisation. But that doesn't mean every gift has to be one-of-a-kind, monogrammed and both a complete surprise and yet exactly what they wanted. Take classic gifts such as flowers as a starting point and personalise it to your boo. What's their style? Would they prefer a dark and dramatic bouquet of poisonous blooms such as lilies and foxgloves? Or would they get into the creativity of a bouquet of origami flowers, folded by yours truly?

Made

WITH

love

171

Like a stake through the heart

Material girls and guys

These generous givers and receivers don't like being accused of being materialistic. Yes, they like to see material demonstrations of your love and affection. But that doesn't mean that they are 'using' their boo or only care about money. They find value in your gifts through the thought you put into the concept and the way you've shown how well you know them.

Thankless

Don't let small gifts fly under the radar. All gifts from a gift giver hold some meaning. If you receive them without saying thank you, then they may feel underappreciated.

All cash, no flash

Let's be honest. A big spend can sweep someone off their feet, regardless of their main love language. However, an expensive gift that has absolutely no connection to your gift-giving boo will leave them cold – even colder than usual. In fact, it may reveal to them that you don't know them well at all. They would prefer something low key and thoughtfully picked rather than a gift that's basically an expensive sign reading, 'I don't know what my boo likes'.

MAIN CHARACTER ENERGY

Pick your gifts and I'll tell you what main character energy you possess.

Hurray! It's your birthday and your boo has got you the perfect present. It is . . .

A: Something shiny, sharp and stabby. Just what you needed.

B: An invite to a date. Spending time with your crush is all you wanted.

C: A hamper of your favourite treats. Awww, how thoughtful.

D: An ancient tome full of dark secrets. This will help put your plots in motion.

Your boo is heading to the shops and asks if you need anything.
Yes, please, you'd like . . .

A: A bundle of wood.
You're racing through your stakes.

B: A surprise.
Whatever your boo chooses will be perfect.

C: A cute toy.
You'd like to add to your collection of goofy geek toys.

D: Arsenic.
No, they can't ask why.

Your boo thought of you while they were on a day trip and came home with a souvenir. You love your new . . .

A: Rune necklace.
Every little bit of protection helps.

B: Photobooth picture of your boo. You'll pin it up with all the other photos.

C: Tacky knick-knack.
It's so weird, you love it!

D: Roadkill.
You have untold uses for the body.

You're excited – your boo has hinted that they've bought you both tickets for your next date. You hope they're for . . .

A: A theme park.
You could really do with some light relief.

B: Your favourite viewpoint. You just want something simple and outdoorsy.

C: A petting zoo.
Yay, fluffy animals!

D: A library of forbidden tomes. The dark knowledge it would contain . . .

RESULTS

Mostly As: You're a badass slay queen. You're tough and outgoing but you have a sweet side. Falling in love with a vampire should be against the rules, but you can't help yourself.

Mostly Bs: You're the babe next door. People write you off as a bit of a wallflower, but you blossom when you spend time with your boo.

Mostly Cs: You are too sweet to be true! You like everything cute and fluffy. It might surprise some people that you've fallen for a vamp, but they're cute to you.

Mostly Ds: You're a deadpan genius. Sarcastic and ambitious. Once you're ready, you might just take over the world.

Make your crush blush

Some people are natural gift givers. Others can't even come up with a birthday list for themselves. If you struggle with gift ideas – for anyone – then it may worry you when you realise it's your boo's idea of ultimate romance. You might be thinking, *Thanks, Crimson. Thanks for letting me know that all I have to do to make my crush happy is find the most perfect, most thoughtful gift every time.*

Don't worry, I'm not going to leave you hanging. Here is my Rosetta Stone for lovers of giving and receiving.

Make a list

Keep a list on your phone and add to it every time your boo mentions they covet something. Every time they say that they've been dying to see a certain musician live or that they've always wanted to do something.

Do they mention that they love cheesy vampire flicks? It goes on the list. Do they mention that a certain snack is their favourite? It goes on the list.

You'll create a massive index of all your boo's likes, loves and dreams, ready for you to tap into whenever you want to buy them a present.

Upgrade them

Gifts don't have to be something completely new and surprising. A really good method of gift giving is to give something your boo already has and likes but upgrade it.

Say your boo is a fan of moodily smudged eyeliner. Do your research and get them the no. 1 smudgy eyeliner (that's within your budget).

Perhaps your crush loves a good witch's brew. Buy them some fancy teabags from the posh witch shop.

Dear Crimson,

What can I get the vamp who has everything? They come from an old, old, old, old, old – you get the idea – family! In vampiric terms, they are the ultimate nepo baby. If they want something, then they buy it themselves. I can't match their budget, so they usually buy nicer things than I can afford. I worry that I'll embarrass myself at their next birthday. Why would they want any of my gifts when they have such cool stuff already?

Yours,

Babe on a Budget

Hey, Babe,

I hear your worries. It's tricky when money gets wrapped up with romance. Whether your boo is a vampire with dusty cellars filled with glamorous antiques or your budget simply doesn't match your ambition, money woes can have you all mixed up.

The act of giving is about so much more than the monetary value. Cliché alert: it really is the thought that counts. If you think that your boo doesn't need any more material objects, then you need to think of another way to give them a gift.

You could give the gift of an experience. Your boo may have cavorted with royalty, but have they ever ridden a ten-loop rollercoaster? Have you ever seen a vampire play crazy golf? How about completing an escape room? Your SO puts the crypt in cryptic clue, so they should really flourish in that environment. For your next big gift-giving opportunity, plan a day trip or buy tickets to something your boo has never tried before. You could even make an event of the gifting, creating a treasure trail or scavenger hunt with clues as to what your gift will be.

Always here to serve.
Crimson

Bloodsucker moment

Your boo keeps plying you with lavish gifts. Are they the bomb, or are they love bombing?

Imagine you have an argument with your partner. It might have been something small, such as despite the fact they have super-strength, they never seem to screw the lid on the condiments correctly. Bam, ketchup everywhere. Or perhaps you're seeing more serious fractures in your relationship. However, every time you approach your boo with the problem of the chasm of immortality that stands between you, the conversation feels strangely unresolved. The next day, you receive a big bouquet of flowers, or they surprise you with an oil painting of yourself. You thought you were about to break up, so when your partner surprises you with an all-expenses-paid trip to the spooky old castle of your dreams, you're taken aback.

You have new clothes, lovely jewellery, pampering trips and everything you've ever – and never – wanted. But, the ketchup lid remains unscrewed. The behaviour that annoyed you is still happening. The differences that you saw between you remain unresolved. Is your boo buying their way out of growing together in the relationship?

Here's how to see through the red mists of passion and the blinding sparkle of fancy jewellery and find out whether you've been love bombed.

- **Are the gifts relevant?** Your boo may have splashed their cash and presented you with a gift that's lavish, jaw-dropping and expensive. But . . . what has that gift got to do with you? Could it have been given to anyone – something big but basic?

- **Are you seeing any changes?** After the argument, and the apology gift, has anything changed? Your partner has said things will be different – do their actions reflect their words? Or are their promises – like a mirror with a vampire standing in front of it – empty?

- **Do they demand more gratitude than necessary?** Love bombers use their lavish gifts to move the needle on the difficult conversations. Now there's pressure to perform a speed run of all the emotions that come with challenging relationship conversations. They guilt trip you for wanting to continue the discussion around the problems you were facing and expect you to show only gratitude for their gift.

Gifts to avoid

Over the years, humans have built secret languages into things you might not ever suspect. There's the language of flowers, which allowed people to send secret messages through bouquets of flowers simply by including certain blossoms. For example, yellow roses meant friendship. By sending a bouquet of yellow roses to someone you're courting, you'd be telling them, 'I just see you as a friend'. In the same way, there is a lot of supernatural lore to wrap your head around when you fall for a vampire. One element of vampire lore is that certain materials that are completely safe for humans can cause vampires great harm.

Tap into this quick guide to materials that can harm vampires, to ensure that the gift you give your boo doesn't send secret messages, such as, 'I'm going to poison you'.

Wood

Everyone knows that a stake through the heart can be deadly to a vampire. To be honest, it wouldn't have many benefits for a human either. I don't think I need to warn you that gifting your boo a wooden stake might be taken as a threatening message.

However, there are some woods that are particularly harmful to vampires. You might want to be aware of them before you pick up a cute little carving on a day trip and gift it to your boo.

- **Ash**
- **Aspen**
- **Hawthorn**
- **Oak**
- **Rosewood**

Silver

Werewolves have a famous aversion to silver. However, did you know that silver can have an adverse effect on many supernatural creatures? Old folklore claimed that it would ward off evil spirits. You may be tempted to buy your boo some jewellery. If so, avoid silver to ensure they don't have an allergic reaction.

Mirrors

Mirrors used to be placed in halls and doorways to ward off evil spirits. If you spot a cute mirror at the local flea market and you think that gilt edging would go perfectly with your crush's high-goth decor, think again. You may think you're sending the message, 'I saw this and thought of you', but your crush might hear, 'Stay away!'

Iron

Iron is one of the two main components of stainless steel, which is one of the most common materials used today. Oh, sorry – have you drifted off? Apologies for the science lesson, but you need to be in the know if you're buying a gift for the witch of your dreams. Lore of old says that witches have an aversion to iron. Although lore of old doesn't have much to say about iron composites, given that stainless steel hadn't been invented yet, it's probably best to avoid it all the same.

Dating disasters

Still not fluent

You're looking at your shelves and feeling confused. When you and your boo deciphered each other's love languages and you both realised that their love language is gift giving and receiving, you didn't exactly have any expectations in mind. You had a vague idea what stereotypical romantic presents were – flowers, chocolates, jewellery. Perhaps they would give them a vampiric twist – roses with the heads lopped off – something along those lines.

However, now you have a small pile of very unexpected gifts lining your shelves. A fossil, a particularly smooth stone, a small sweet treat from a town they visited, a lock of fur from a defeated werewolf nemesis. What exactly are you supposed to do with this pile of seemingly unconnected knick-knacks?

Further translation is needed!

This form of the gift giving love language is sometimes known as pebbling. It involves your crush giving you small gifts with

very little monetary value, but lots of sentimental value. For example, they may have gone for a midnight stroll and seen something that reminded them of you. And that is how you end up with a pressed flower that may or may not have come from someone's graveside. This is their way of saying that they are always thinking of you. They are also communicating that they want you to feel the same pleasure they felt when they saw something charming, whimsical, dangerous, beautiful – pick the adjective that you feel applies to you.

Some gift receivers feel confused by gifts that they can't 'do' something with or that so clearly have no monetary value. However, others will understand the message behind it.

ALL MY LOVE...

Fangs for reading! Whether you're happily boo'd up or single and seeking, I'm A-positive that you'll have come away from this book with new tools in your arsenal. Maybe I've helped you shine a light on why your heart skips a beat when your SO returns home with a treat for you in their back pocket. Maybe you finally understand why you can talk about your feelings until midnight but others aren't so keen. It's possible that you've realised you're a hybrid – you're into quality time as a love language but you also have a strong focus on acts of service.

Whether you identify closely with words of affirmation, quality time, acts of service, gift giving and receiving or physical touch, knowing your own mind is just the start. You don't want to rush into a relationship with a bloodsucker without first knowing yourself (advice Bella Swan should have taken). In fact, you might like to read through this book again with your supernatural someone or your ghoulfriends, so you can discover your love languages as a couple or group.

You may encounter bumps in the road as you take the first steps on the path to true love, or maybe you want to build strong foundations before trouble starts rocking the relationship. Perhaps you've asked for more romance in your relationship but feel confused about why your vampiric SO has started dropping werewolves on your doorstep like a cat drops mice? Either way, I hope this book has been the dating guide you needed to read.

And remember, love languages aren't just to help you catch a girlfriend or boyfriend. Understanding the way a person shows their affection, and their priorities, will help you build strong and healthy relationships with everyone in your life, from your friends to your family. And they'll save you from wasting your time on life-draining ghouls and serial ghosters.

So enjoy exploring your love languages and dating the Edwards and Jacobs of the world. Just make sure not to fall in love at first bite!

Crimson x

IF YOU LIKED THIS WHY NOT TRY . . .

MAIN CHARACTER ENERGY

Jordan Paramor

ROMANTICISE YOUR LIFE and PUT YOURSELF FIRST

Natalie Hutchinson

MANIFEST Your Dreams

Your beginner's toolkit for MANIFESTING in 10 easy steps

JEAN MENZIES
ILLUSTRATED BY TAYLOR DOLAN

LIVE LIKE A GODDESS

LIFE LESSONS FROM LEGENDS AND LORE